The Boys from Clyde

*Sherwood Anderson, Henry Bardshar, Karl Anderson
Herman Hurd, Cliff Paden*

Dorothy Davis Cox

✳ ✳ ✳

Clyde Heritage League
Clyde, Ohio

The Boys from Clyde is based on accounts of actual events
in Clyde, Ohio printed in the *Clyde Enterprise* and other
contemporaneous sources.
Dorothy Davis Cox
Illustrations by Dorothy Davis Cox
Copyright 2014 Clyde Heritage League Inc.
All rights reserved.
No part of this book may be used or reproduced in any manner
whatsoever without the written permission of the Publisher
Printed in the United States of America.
For information write to 124 West Buckeye Street, Clyde OH 43410

clydeheritageleague.org

ISBN: 978-0-692-27535-1

Contents

Onward and Upward	1
Adventures with Spondulkies	33
Growing Up, Moving On	65
Busy Times in Town	99
The Clyde Boys	131
Later Years	159

Onward and Upward

Rain lashed the upper windows of the Nichols Hotel, soaking the rooftops, and the blustery March wind whipped sheets of water across the desolate street below. Tin advertising signs rattled and loose tree branches littered the hotel yard.

Sherwood Anderson in his nightshirt stood at the window looking out at the bleak landscape and sobbed. He was seven years old.

The sobs woke his brother, Karl.

"What's the matter?" he asked.

Karl was ten. He slipped out from the lumpy mattress and went to comfort his little brother.

"My puppy is gone," Sherwood whimpered. He rubbed the sleeve of his nightshirt across his wet eyes.

"Papa said he'd get you another, bigger and better," Karl said.

Both boys knew better. It was one of their father's stock phrases.

Emma, their mother, entered the room with a white washbowl and pitcher to wash and inspect behind their ears.

"Hush," she said. "You'll wake the baby."

"Come downstairs when you're dressed."

Karl buttoned his jacket and waited for Sherwood to tie his shoes. He stood at the window, looking at rain-drenched Main Street, the dismal shops of the town, the bleak atmosphere. He felt trapped.

In Caledonia, the day before had dawned cold and gray. It had rained through the night, and patches of puddles in the street reflected the somber sky.

Over the past few years, the Anderson family had moved from Morning Sun to Camden to Independence to Caledonia, and now they were moving to Clyde.

"Cap, it's hard to believe you're actually going to move away from Caledonia," one of the townspeople said to I. M. Anderson.

"Clyde, Ohio. That's the place to be," the Captain answered, hands in his pockets, hat cocked back on his head. "Onward and upward. Opportunities of a lifetime. It's the town for us. Life will be sweeter there, I'm sure of it."

"About how big a place is Clyde?" one of the villagers asked.

"I'd say the population is probably 2000, 2500 or so," the Captain said. "Bigger and better. Onward and upward." The population of Caledonia was less than 700.

Inside the railway depot, the Anderson family waited for the early morning train. A pot-bellied stove warmed the waiting room. The train was late. Emma, in her flowered hat and Sunday best, sat near the stove and cradled baby Ray on her lap. Karl, the oldest, lingered nearby. He was in charge of the bags and bundles. Stella, next oldest and only girl, tended to a restless Irve who was prancing a make-believe pony up and down in front of the benches.

One of the neighbors had given Sherwood a puppy and it was squirming in his arms.

"Hold still, you little puppy dog," Sherwood commanded, shifting the struggling pup.

Sensing an opportunity to escape, the dog gave one forceful squirm and leaped out of Sherwood's arms.

People were in and out of the depot waiting for the train, the outside doors opening and closing. The pup bolted through the open station doors and was off like lightning down the street. It sped past the shops of the town and ran back toward the Anderson's vacated house, splashing water from the puddles.

Sherwood raced down the sloppy street in search of the puppy.

"Sherwood! Sherwood, come back here!" Emma called. She turned to her husband. "Irwin, Sherwood has run after that dog."

The Captain, in animated conversation with the men gathered around the station and expounding on the glories of the bright future that lay ahead, paid little attention to his family.

"I'll go get him, Ma," Karl said, and headed down the street.

He found his brother under the porch of their abandoned house, looking for the run-away pup. Far off a train whistle sounded.

"Come on out of there, Sherwood. The train's coming," Karl said.

"I'm not going!"

"Oh, yes you are. Ma sent me after you."

Karl grabbed his brother by the legs and pulled him from under the porch. Sherwood wiggled loose, scrambled to his feet and dashed away again. Karl caught up with him with a few strides and grabbed his jacket. The boys scuffled. The jacket ripped. Sherwood stumbled and fell in the soft damp red dirt. Again the train whistle blew, and it sounded closer this time.

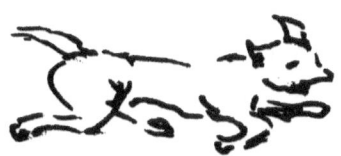

"Come on Sherwood. Ma's gonna be mad enough."

"I can't find my puppy," Sherwood sobbed, tears streaking his face.

Karl put his arm around his younger brother's shoulder and gently led him back to the train station.

Emma Anderson lifted the baby onto Stella's lap while she pulled a handkerchief from her bag, moistened it with spittle, and dabbed at Sherwood's face.

Karl brushed at his jacket and pants with his hand, trying to get some of the dirt off. He only made it worse.

Emma examined Sherwood's torn jacket and sighed. She tightened her lips, but she didn't scold.

The Captain, on the platform with the men, saw the train down the track, checked in his vest pocket for his tickets, and went inside the station to round up his family. He took no notice of the boys' appearance. "Let's go," he said. "Train's here."

Sherwood was crying again. "Papa, my puppy is gone. I can't find him."

"No matter, Son," the Captain said, "When we get to Clyde, I'll get you another dog. A bigger and better one."

It was evening when the train reached Clyde, Ohio. The Captain, Emma, and their brood, laden with their belongings, disheveled, tired and hungry, struggled into the Nichols House lobby. Behind the desk sat a little gray-haired man in a felt hat and a quizzical expression on his face.

"What can I do for you folks?" he asked as he leaned his folded arms on the desk. The Captain stepped forward and stuck out his hand.

"Captain--" He stopped himself, and without missing a beat, gave himself a promotion. "Major Anderson, here. Well, sir, a bite of supper for the family and accommodations for the night."

On Monday, June 30, 1884, a couple of Frenchmen appeared on the streets of Clyde with an immense ugly bear. Boys followed them, poked the bear with sticks, pulled his hair and tormented him. The bear quietly submitted for a time, but finally it became provoked and took Willie Sargeant in his arms and hugged and squeezed him. Willie kicked and screamed. Fortunately, the bear was muzzled. Willie was lucky. He only got a few scratches.

At the height of the excitement, Mayor Henry Paden came upon the scene. He told the boys to scatter.

Instead, the men and the bear were the ones to flee the situation.

"Hold on." Mayor Paden called after them. "Where is your permit to exhibit on our streets? You have no permission to be here."

A posse started in hot pursuit of the men and the bear and they were brought back, given a hearing and fined $10 each and costs, making it $27.40. This they said they did not have and in default of payment they were committed to the village lock-up.

It seems that after reflecting on the situation, they paid the fine and were allowed to go in their way.

"So Pa told the Frenchmen to take their bear and get out of town," Cliff Paden told the boys.

Karl and Sherwood Anderson, Herman Hurd and Cliff were among the boys gathered at the depot along Main Street near the Lake Shore railroad crossing.

"Willie Sargeant's always doing something he shouldn't," Sherwood said.

❋ ❋ ❋

One day in January, 1885 when Karl, Sherwood, Herman and Cliff were walking home from school, they heard what sounded like a fight. They ended up at the Lake Shore depot where they crouched just below the loading platform to see what was going on.

"You know them?" Sherwood whispered to Cliff.

"Yeah, Wesley Burroughs. Lives over by the organ factory. He's one of 'em. The others is Peters. Leonard Peters, I think. He's in trouble all the time."

There was a little dog nipping at the heels of the first one, then the other of the men. The men were going at each other with their fists and cursing back and forth. Not much later, the constable came by, swinging his nightstick, grabbed the men by their collars and hustled them off to jail.

"That's either an assault or a Breach of Peace," Cliff said.

"Wow," Sherwood said.

"They'll have to go up before Pa. He'll charge them and they'll have to pay a fine before they can get out of jail."

"Where did you learn all this stuff, Cliff?" Karl asked.

"From my Pa. He's got a big book of Village Ordinances and Crimes and how much the fines are," Cliff said.

"So what was it, Cliff?" Sherwood asked a few days later.

"What was what?" Cliff had no idea what Sherwood was talking about.

Sherwood had mulled the fight over in his mind, wondering about it and the men. Was it some kind of quarrel? About family? About money?"

"The fight we saw last Monday. Those two fellows. Did your Pa fine them?" Sherwood clarified the incident for Cliff.

"Oh, that," Cliff said off hand, "Pa fined 'em four dollars each. They paid up and they were discharged."

"Ha!" What was it about?"

"It was all about a dog," Cliff said.

"Ha!" Sherwood said again.

"Yeah, my dad gets lots of strange cases. The other day Pa sentenced a fellow to twenty days in jail."

"What for?"

"It was J.N. I don't know his name. Pa just calls him, J.N. He's always doing something illegal."

Cliff relished his audience. He teased and dramatized his presentation, enjoying his audience.

"You know where the jail is?"

Sherwood nodded.

"You know the little window at the back of the jail?"

Sherwood nodded, impatient to get on with it.

"Old J.N. was smuggling whiskey to the prisoners in the jail through that little window."

"Wow," Sherwood said.

"So J.N. got twenty days and the jail window got boarded up."

✳ ✳ ✳

About five o'clock on Tuesday evening, February 10th, 1885, the Village Hall bell rang out the alarm of fire. One of Clyde's newest, prettiest and most substantial dwelling houses caught fire. It was the Harkness Lay home on Cherry Street, not far from Main. The house was built with an upright part, two stories high with a wing of the same height, and a back kitchen with an attic over it.

The fire department was on hand in record time with a supply of water from the waterworks. When the firemen first arrived, flames were lapping at the cornice around the kitchen. Dense clouds of smoke poured from the upper story of the upright section.

A large crowd gathered despite the zero temperature. While the firemen arranged their hoses, the onlookers turned their attention to saving the contents of the house. It was evident that efforts to save the house would be fruitless. All of the furniture on the first floor was carried out, but upstairs the smoke was so dense that the men could not see and they had to abandon the contents.

The fire started in the attic over the kitchen and the firemen had a difficult time reaching it. The fire burned through to the outside, licking up everything in its way. The roof burned through to the lower story. What furniture was left upstairs was ruined by water and

falling debris. The water froze wherever it fell, covering the men with sheets of ice. The ladies came out in the inclement weather and distributed hot coffee and hot soups to the men.

The boys, Karl, Sherwood, Herman Hurd, and Cliff went down later and looked at the burnt out residence. Cliff told them about the fire. Harkness Lay was Cliff's uncle.

"Uncle Hark said that at first everyone thought it was started from the stump of a lighted match. They thought my cousin Frank had been hunting for something and lit a match in the attic and then threw it on the floor."

"Wow," Karl said.

"But wait." Cliff held up his hands. "It turns out that no fire reached the part of the house where Frank dropped the match. So now, they don't know what started it. We've got a houseful of people- Uncle Hark, Aunt Nett, and my cousins Frank and Bessie."

"You've got a big family to begin with," the Anderson brothers commented.

"Not only that, but my brother Fred's home from Georgia. He's been in military school there. So we are bulging at the seams and we don't know for how long."

With all the snow and zero weather it's pretty tough," the boys added.

"And-" Cliff added, "I hate to think what my cousin Frankie'll say."

The fire was a major topic of conversation in town for weeks. High praise was bestowed upon the McPherson Hook and Ladder Company and the Clyde Engine Company. Fighting a fire is not an easy task in ideal weather, but when the mercury drops below zero, fighting a fire is not pleasant. All hands remained at their posts and many had frozen ears, fingers and feet before the flames subdued.

"Pa says the waterworks proved a godsend," Cliff related to the boys. "If we hadn't had the plentiful supply of water from the waterworks, not only Uncle Hark's house would have burnt to the ground, but the houses on all sides would have burned, too."

Herman Hurd agreed.

"Both of our houses, included," he said to Cliff. "Maybe all of Cherry Street. There was a strong west wind, which made fighting the fire worse than ever."

Cliff sighed. "Pa says this fire is a warning. It could have been worse. And what the town needs to do is to have council pass legislation and enlarge the capacity of the reservoir and to extend the water pipes to all streets in town."

"Good idea." The boys all exclaimed.

"Pa says iron pipe is cheap now and there are plenty of able-bodied men lying idle who can do the work, earn some money," Cliff said.

He went on. "Pa says a few years ago there was a proposal to buy a steamer for the protection of our town against fire. Certain citizens called it an expensive plaything. Later on, when the proposition came up to establish a system of waterworks, these same croakers did all they could to defeat the plan. Now we have seen our steam fire engine save buildings from utter ruin."

Cliff was proud of his father. He constantly quoted him to any who would listen. And Henry Paden, Mayor of Clyde, was full of good suggestions. He asked that the matter of extension of the waterworks be put on the ballot for April so that Clyde would be ready for any emergency.

The Major was interested in the talk of the waterworks expansion, but he did not want to get involved. After all, there was a dance at the Opera House coming up in another week and Miller's City Band would play.

✻ ✻ ✻

The boys of Clyde were always interested in hearing the latest from Cliff about the goings on around town. Cliff relished telling them all he knew.

Peter Hubert, or "Smoky Pete" as he was known was picked up in February for using obscene language in the presence and hearing of females. He was sentenced to twenty days in the county jail at Fremont. He returned and was greeted warmly by old friends and the marshal of Clyde.

"But for Clyde, the sheriff could not live," Pete told them. "Of the five prisoners in jail, three were from Clyde."

Pete went on to say that Sheriff Pohlman had been expecting him so that he could have the jail cell whitewashed. Pete laughed. "He knows my habits well." Pete said. "There's no place on earth I hate more than the inside of the Clyde calaboose since the high fence was put up in front of the door and windows."

The calaboose was built at rear of Village Hall about fifteen years ago. It was little more than a wooden shack, but had iron doors and iron grating over the small windows. Pranksters nailed a sign, Brown's Hotel, over the door in honor of LeRoy Brown's father, who was the town marshal at the time. The jail housed mostly drunks sleeping it off. Smoky Pete was a frequent guest.

Pete was a popular fellow when he was sober and a good wood sawyer. But he warned everyone, "When I make up my mind to go on a 'jamboree,' go I will, and send me to Fremont."

"Pete, do you know what's coming up?"

Pete said he didn't.

"April 7th is Election Day," was the answer.

"Jamboree, here I come," Smoky Pete answered.

❋ ❋ ❋

It was a Thursday, May 14, 1885. Sherwood and Herman Hurd were discussing the incident that happened at school.

"Old Man Ginn whipped Willie hard!" Herman said.

"Willie was just having a little fun," Sherwood answered, and then he paused. "I'd just like to know how Willie tied that string to the bee in the first place."

"Me too," Herman said.

Willie Sargeant was in the same class as Herman and Sherwood. He had a live white-headed bee tied to a string in the schoolhouse and was tormenting the girls with the bee. Naturally someone told and Superintendent Ginn punished Willie, whipping him just below the knees on his bare legs.

"Look at my legs," Willie cried, "All these red lines. I'm gonna tell my Pa!"

John Sargeant, Willie's father, who was the marble dealer and who had the contract to put in the sawed stone sidewalk at the school confronted the school board. He wrote them a letter and demanded that the board reprimand Ginn.

"The boy deserved the punishment," Ginn said. "I was merely punishing the lad for an inexcusable incident. I used a very small peach tree sprout, and naturally it's going to leave a mark."

The board issued a statement: 'It is our opinion that the boy deserved punishment but that he should not have been punished on the bare legs and would respectfully suggest that the superintendent be cautioned against too severe punishing.'

The bumblebee incident was the topic of discussion among the boys of the town.

"I told you old fakir Ginn was mean," Cliff reminded them.

"Fakir Ginn punished Willie and the school board punished fakir Ginn," one of the boys commented.

"The School Board," Herman Hurd mused, "has power over the Superintendent."

※ ※ ※

One of the pastimes of the boys in Clyde was to watch workers. Buildings were being erected all over town. The Grace Episcopal Church on West Buckeye near Main was one. Ground had been broken on October 12, 1885. The design was a frame structure with a slate roof and was drawn by architect J. C. Johnson of Fremont. Charles Wolf of Ballville had the contract for the superstructure.

Mayor Paden was one of the early promoters of the church. He had put in his ideas as to design and purpose.

"The audience room should be large, fifty by thirty feet at the most, and the extreme length of the building should be 74 feet. There should be an arched and vaulted roof and a commodious chancel nave for the choir and a vestry room in addition to the audience room."

Cliff and Karl stood at the edge of the excavation and observed the activity.

"Imagine preaching a sermon in this new church," Cliff said.

"No. I can't imagine," Karl said.

※ ※ ※

The Andersons had lived on South Main Street, Duane Street and now in 1886 had moved again. The house on Mechanic Street was a modest two-story dwelling with a long front porch. The Bardshar family lived next door in a huge square house, which was perched on the edge of an embankment. The vast backyard had been an abandoned gravel pit. There was an odd assortment of buildings on the property: sheds, chicken coops, a stable and a hogpen. There was a barn where the neighborhood boys gathered in the haymow on a rainy Sunday afternoon to play cards.

"Aw, Ma, what's so sinful about Euchre or Old Maid?" Henry asked his mother when she reprimanded him for playing cards on Sunday.

The Bardshar basement opened out into the ground level pit. Henry had his own workshop in the basement. He had scrounged around and found worn out tools and lost back-alley treasures. Henry was a tinkerer and envisioned a multitude of ways to make money.

The Bardshar place fascinated the boys of Clyde. The backyard was littered with rusty farm machinery, remnants of carriages and broken down wagons. The boys would climb on the abandoned equipment, pretend to ride off into the West and capture Indians. Henry portrayed the leader of a caravan crossing the plains with his trusty rifle across his arms, ready to slay the hidden Indian.

❋ ❋ ❋

In May, 1886, the workers were putting finishing touches on the Grace Episcopal Church. Karl, Cliff and Henry had stopped by on their way home from school. They took the long way home.

Some of the men were taking down ladders, closing up paint cans, washing brushes, doing the normal clean-up. The boys had been regulars at the construction site whether they attended school or not and they were a bit sorry to see the building completed.

"Don't worry. Plenty of new buildings going up. Chester Hunter is building a tool factory next to Arnold & Vanator's Mill – the Star Mill and they are starting on the Catholic Church," one of the workmen told the boys, "That will be a big one."

"Too close to the school to suit me," Henry said.

The sky was clouding up and turning dark. Early leaves were rustling and trees were swaying in the west wind. The air was warm, but it was jacket weather.

"A storm is brewing, lads. Better get along home," one of the workmen called to the boys.

They all headed north on Main Street to walk Cliff to the depot. Mrs. Weissert's store at Main and Railroad had a new stone sidewalk. The boys inspected it. Mrs. Weissert came to the door.

"You boys best be getting on home. There's a storm coming," she said.

The wind was flapping the awning. The boys liked Mrs. Weissert. She was carrying on after the death of her husband. She stocked a supply of groceries, country produce, confectionery and notions. Since Cliff was the one with the cash in his pocket, he sometimes treated his friends.

Down Railroad Street at the Nichols House, some workers had finished a new plank walk. The boys tested it out. Rowena Baker came to the door of the City Bakery where she was the proprietress. Her bakery was the first door east of the Nichols House. Her daughter, Jennie came and stood by her mother.

"Just admiring the new plank walk, Mrs. Baker," Karl said. He recognized Jennie as a girl in Sherwood's class. Mrs. Baker wiped her hands on her apron.

"I've been watching the sky," she said. "It's going to be a bad storm. Your mothers will be worried."

"Yes, Maam. We're heading home," Henry said.

After helping Cliff get his papers in order and taken care of and telling each other to 'hurry it up...there was a storm coming'. They went on toward Mechanic Street cutting across back yards and jumping fences on the way.

Emma Anderson and Ruth Bardshar watched down the street. The wind was tearing at the shutters of the houses and swinging unlatched doors back and forth, banging them against the houses. Karl and Henry came racing up the street. The storm hit as they reached their houses. The wind battered the back porch and blew sheets of rain across Mechanic Street creating large pools of water. The air turned ice cold.

People had let their coal fires go out and most of the townspeople felt the need of stove heat on Saturday and Sunday. The Major, on the other hand, stoked up the coal heater in the front room and before long the house was comfortable.

The Major gave a sly laugh. "Sure you've been wanting me to take this stove down for weeks, Emma. Now for once, I believe you're a lee-tle bit glad I'm lazy."

Once again, the Major, with a fake Scottish brogue charmed Emma. How could she be upset that he hadn't dismantled the coal stove when all the neighbors had packed theirs away for the summer.

The storm was disastrous. It ruined crops and tore down partial constructions and downed trees. Sucker Run and Coon Creek were over the banks in places. And mud was everywhere.

"When they gonna macadamize Main Street?" was Smoky Pete's cry.

❋ ❋ ❋

The boys, Karl and Sherwood Anderson and Henry Bardshar were all interested in horses. The horse was a necessary means of transportation, and there were stables and barns at many homes. Others, who didn't own horses, rented them from the livery stables. Hitching posts and rails were standard equipment downtown. New wooden hitching posts with iron rails had been erected in front of Kline's block.

B.F. Heffner was an auctioneer in Clyde. He was partial to farm sales, especially horses.

"Best sale I cried this season," he told the mayor, "Sold John Hilbish's property over by Bellevue. One horse sold for $950, another for $346 and a third for $301."

"Horses are going for a good price, I guess," said one of the townsmen.

"Good horses are," Ben said.

The two discussed business around Clyde. Another horse trader, Tom Whitehead had a stable north of Clyde. He was an Englishman in his mid-thirties, a dealer, who owned racehorses. He had just sold one of his thoroughbred horses to an eastern buyer.

"Tom got a fancy price for it." B.F. Heffner said.

The boys rode Henry's old nag out to watch the horse auctions.

"I'd sure like to get enough money to get me a good horse," Henry said, "I'm going to think about how we could make some money.

***

The Grace Episcopal Church on Buckeye was now completed, and the first service was Friday, May 21st, 1886. The audience room was filled to capacity. Everyone was anxious to see and take part whether they were members or not.

"We may need more seats," Mayor Paden said. "Reverend Hamilton is going to deliver the baccalaureate sermon before the graduating class here on June 6th."

The talk before and after the services was of the storm last week.

"Paper said Ohio farmers lost seven million dollars from that storm," one of the parishioners reported.

"Strawberry crop looks good. Plants are low to the ground. If we get a few days of hot sunshine, the berry crop will flourish," said another.

By Memorial Day, the mud of Main Street had turned to dust. Clouds of dust whipped by the horses hooves and the wind caused much discomfort to both the marchers and the onlookers.

VanDoren's Drum Corps led the parade. The Citizen's Band, which made its first appearance played appropriate music, "Yankee Doodle" and "Rally Round the Flag."

The program and parade followed much the same pattern as in other years. School children joined in the procession. Ceremonies were held at McPherson Cemetery. The Major rode a white horse.

Sherwood and Karl were walking home. Sherwood was full of ideas and Karl was patiently listening to his younger brother.

"I want to make a lot of money, Karl, so I can buy things."

Karl asked where he thought he could get a job and if he had any money, what would he buy?

One thing Sherwood was sure he could get a paper delivery job like Cliff Paden, but that would have to be when he was older – or he could pick strawberries now.

"I want to get a silver watch like Cliff's got," Sherwood said.

"In the first place, it isn't silver," Karl said, "Its nickel plated and the plate's partly worn off. He showed me."

Sherwood said he didn't care. Karl told him Cliff needed a watch. He needed to be at the depot when his papers came in." Karl laughed. "But he pays no attention to the time school starts. Even the second bell. He's always late." Then Karl paused. They walked about a half block in silence.

"None of this matters anyway," Karl went on. "Cliff lost his watch last week. I guess he's putting an ad in the *Enterprise*."

"So, I think I'll pick strawberries out to Wellivers down on Vine by the railroad. He'll be looking for pickers," Sherwood said.

Wagonloads of crates of strawberries were driven out of Clyde to the cities. American Express Company shipped berries out of town and since the first of June, the United Express Company had shipped 749 crates of strawberries. They did such a flourishing business that the company had to install a new safe.

The boys of Clyde including the Anderson brothers joined the pickers and were out in the patch after the sun had dried the dew. They worked until late in the morning when the patch was cleaned of ripe berries and baskets and containers all turned in. Their backs ached and their feet and knees tingled from all the walking and bending and squatting over the rows of berries. Their fingers were pink and sore.

"Maybe Ma will make a strawberry shortcake for supper," Karl chuckled to Sherwood, teasing him.

Sherwood rolled his eyes. He had eaten two berries for every one he picked when they started out. But later, the taste of the berries wore off and both boys buckled down to picking more than they ate. They felt rich with the jingle of the coins in their pockets.

"So, got enough to get a silver watch like Cliff's?" Karl asked.

Sherwood didn't answer. It was going to take longer than he had planned.

***

In the spring when the ground was ready and the weather moderate, the boys of Clyde helped plant cabbage plants. Sherwood and Irve and some of their friends traipsed out to the farms and set cabbage plants in the wet, soggy earth.

"I believe this is worse than picking strawberries," Irve said.

The boys were chilled, their feet numb from the cold.

"I don't believe I'll ever be able to hold my back straight again," Irve said, "I think it's broken."

***

Hark Lay and Henry Paden had pushed for the waterworks extension after the disastrous fire at the Lay place. The pipe laying was completed.

"They'll test the pipes after the fair is over," Paden said, "Now, the town should be ready for any fire emergency."

***

"Spondulkies. That's what Henry said, Karl." Sherwood ran into the house. "Come on, Karl! Hurry up."

The boys usually walked to school together. Henry was a few years older and a classmate of Karl's.

"I'm a fellow with ideas, Karl. Spondulkies. And we're gonna get 'em," Henry said as they walked along.

"What's Spondulkies?" Sherwood asked.

"That's money," Karl explained. "Jingle, jangle in your pocket. What's the plan, Henry?"

Henry pulled a square of red material out of his pocket. "It's plush; a piece of Ma's old curtains. We'll cut cloth into squares like this and make pincushions."

"Pincushions?" the boys repeated.

"Not just any old pincushions, but fancy, very unusual parlor pincushions."

Henry grew excited. He leaped over the backyard fence in Ginn's backyard. The boys usually took a shortcut to school. At the end of Mechanic, they cut across Cherry Street through Gillett's yard, and Superintendent Ginn's to Buckeye, across Maple to the Union School on Vine. Henry whooped and hollered and ran in circles in Ginn's back yard.

"Quiet down, Henry. Old Fakir Ginn'll be after us."

Henry put a finger to his lips, quieting himself and with mincing steps, pranced back to the brothers.

"I can't help it. This is the best idea I've had yet."

He explained how they would make these ornaments.

"They'll be cow's horns filled with sand with the red plush over the top for pins to stick into. Then we'll fasten a ribbon around it to hang it up. Go door to door. Sell 'em and make lots of Spondulkies."

The boys walked along: Henry prancing and dancing; Karl deep in thought and Sherwood puzzled.

"Spondulkies. Spondulkies." Sherwood murmured, mostly to himself.

"You're awful quiet, Karl."

"I'm trying to picture this pincushion," Karl said.

Early Saturday morning the boys gathered in Henry's workshop. He had assembled some heavy twine, knives and an old saw. He unhitched his old raw-boned roan from the stable.

"First stop is the slaughter house. Hop on," Henry said as he led his horse across the yard.

"You can't go this time, Sherwood," Karl said, "You can help when we get back."

"No," Sherwood said, "I planned on this too. You need me."

"Let him come, Karl," Henry said as he leaned over and grabbed Sherwood's arm, hoisting him up on the horse. The three boys astride the old horse rode down Mechanic Street out past the fairgrounds and beyond to the slaughter-house. It was a chilly fall day and the roan kept up a steady clip clop as they rode out into the country.

"There it is," Henry called.

The boys dismounted on the rail fence and tied the horse to it. The field behind the slaughter-house was littered with cattle skulls.

"Sherwood, you run, fetch the skulls. Bring 'em here. I'll saw off the horns and Karl, you tie 'em together so we can get 'em home."

Sherwood ran off across the field slapping his thighs and galloping. Karl and Henry took turns sawing off the horns. It was more difficult than either had imagined. After a long morning's work, Henry wiped his brow. "Lets call it a day."

Karl tied the horns together with twine and slung the string around his shoulders.

"You look like an Indian with a necklace of big teeth," Henry laughed.

"Indians. Indians. That's all you think of, Henry."

"Yes," Henry said, "I'm goin West one day and fight the Indians."

Henry untied the horse and helped Sherwood climb on. He handed Sherwood the saw and then he mounted the fidgety animal.

"Hey, old fellah. What's the trouble?" Henry patted his horse. "You're awful skittish."

Karl stood on the fence waiting for Henry to ride close so he could jump on. Each time Henry rode near Karl, the horse ran away. Finally, Karl made a giant leap and landed on the horse behind Sherwood. The sound of the clattering horns and the suddenness of the jump, startled the horse. He sprinted up the steep embankment and raced down the pike.

"Whoa, Whoa," the boys hollered, holding on to the horse's mane, to the reins and to each other. Henry's cries were the loudest.

"Stop. Stop. Sherwood, drop the saw!"

Sherwood ignored everything and clung to the saw.

Somewhere in the tangle of taking off for home, the saw was turned so that the teeth were against Henry. With every clatter and rattle of the cattle horns, the horse ran faster. With every jump of the horse, Henry's cries became more anguished. In the confusion of Henry's commands to 'Drop it', Karl dropped the cattle horns. The string became loosened and the horns scattered in every direction.

The trio on the horse came barreling down Main Street. Cliff Paden and several other school friends of the boys heard the hoof beats and ran to meet the galloping horse. One of the merchants hurried out of his shop, his apron flapping. He waved his arms at the speeding animal.

Suddenly, the horse came to an abrupt halt. One by one, the boys flew over the animal's head and landed on Main Street. They were shaken up but unhurt.

After Henry caught his horse, he led it back to Mechanic Street. The boys were silent. They were exhausted from the morning adventure, disappointed and embarrassed about their arrival on Main Street.

"We could try again. It's still a good idea. We could go back and pick up the horns." Karl was trying to reassure Henry.

"Nah. Somehow, I'm not so excited about that idea anymore."

"I keep thinking about the Spondulkies, Henry," Sherwood said.

"Yeah," Henry said, "We'll think of something."

"I'm gonna be a newspaper boy like Cliff."

"Yeah?" Karl and Henry were not surprised. Sherwood had mentioned this before.

"He's still thinking about that nickel plated watch," Karl thought.

❋ ❋ ❋

School was out. The day was warm and sunny. Huge maple trees shaded the village streets. Karl was barefoot and the sawed stone sidewalks felt smooth and cool as he walked along.

A tennis ball rolled by him into Buckeye Street. Karl ran and picked it up. Two young men in white flannels were playing tennis on the side lawn of Superintendent Ginn's house. They were his sons, Frank, home from Kenyon College for the summer, and Doctor Arthur, visiting from Fremont.

Karl handed the ball to Frank. He watched them play for a while and walked on. The image of the two young gentlemen in their white outfits playing tennis remained with Karl. This was not an ordinary sight on the lawns of Clyde.

***

Karl and Cliff bantered back and forth on their way home from town. About the organ grinder, who was in Clyde with no monkey, creating a great deal of noise and passing his hat. About William Miller, the merchant tailor's new establishment in Terry's block.

"And speaking of Terry's," Cliff said, "Wow, is that opera hall looking good!"

"What are you talking about, Cliff?" Karl asked.

"I watched the fellows moving stuff upstairs, Karl. They're scenic artists from Chicago. They put up curtains and drapery and new scenery."

"Slow down, Cliff," Karl said. "Who did you say they were?"

"The trunks and crates and boxes all said, 'Douglas and Co.' I was poking around."

A delivery wagon approached them in the street. The boys waved and Cliff waited until the noisy rattle of the wheels and hoof beats of the horses passed by.

"Well, I'm curious. I watched all the unloading and directions given. This man introduced himself as Mr. Walt M. Squire. He had a fine outfit of clothes and a hat like the Englishmen wear. You've seen pictures."

Karl nodded.

"And a gold chain attached to his watch. And a walking stick. He pointed the stick where he wanted something done and these men followed his orders."

"You could get yourself in a peck of trouble, Cliff," Karl said.

"Nah," Cliff said, "No harm in watching and asking questions. You should be more adventurous. More like your brother, Sherwood."

"Oh, sure," Karl said.

Cliff continued. "I watched these men. I went back in a couple of days. Thought maybe I could get a job, but they had all the help they needed. Mr. Squire said they have furnished some of the best halls in the country with curtains and scenery. Let me tell you, Terry's Opera House is elegant. I walked across the stage and looked out across where the seats are and whew, what a feeling! Karl, you've got to go see that opera house."

✱ ✱ ✱

In late August Cliff Paden was badly burned on his arms. He was handling gasoline and it ignited. Sherwood and Karl went over to see him.

"I got Harry Rhodes to take my place," Cliff said to the brothers. He explained, "He only lives down the street and he's made the rounds with me before. Besides, he's older, Sherwood."

"I could do it," Sherwood said.

"You probably could," Cliff was sympathetic to Sherwood's pleas, but since Harry had substituted for him before, he felt he was obligated to Harry. "School starts Monday. Vacation is over so you should have enough homework to keep you busy," Cliff said.

"Homework doesn't pay me money," Sherwood said.

When the school year began in September 1885, Karl Anderson found himself in the same class as his sister, Stella. She was a bright girl and had been moved up a grade. Along with them in the same class were Cliff, Willie Wilder and Henry Bardshar. Henry was two years older, but had been kept back a grade. He was absent as much as he attended school.

Sherwood was two grades behind his brother and sister. He was in a class along with Herman Hurd, Willie

Sargeant, Johnny Botsford, Clarence Whittaker and Moody Dwight.

Cliff was still sore after his accident. The burn areas were painful. He healed slowly, but attended school and also took care of his newspaper delivery service. What was uppermost on his mind was the health of his father. Hy Paden had been seriously ill and announced he was no longer going to be in his office every night.

Henry Bardshar came from a large family. He often told of the family trips to the West and back. Just the past August there was a wedding at the Bardshar's. Nellie, who had been in Kansas, had met a Mr. T. C. McConnell who was in the music business. After the wedding, they returned to Kansas. Henry's sister, Frona, also a traveler, was home a while before starting her fall teaching at the school on North Ridge.

❈ ❈ ❈

Cliff's Uncle Hark Lay's house was completely finished and remodeled.

"It's as handsome as it was before it burned down," he said.

The ladies of the Episcopal Society held a chicken-pie social at the Lay residence. The supper was twenty-five cents. Friends and the general public would have a chance to have their supper and admire the improvements.

Jennie Baker was in Sherwood and Herman Hurd's class. Her mother, Mrs. Henry Baker purchased the City Bakery several years ago. Now, she planned to add an ice cream parlor and a full line of spices, candies, cigars and tobacco. The boys of Clyde patronized her place when they had a few pennies to spend.

✳ ✳ ✳

Beginning in late August and continuing through the fall, horse races featuring trotting took place on Wednesdays and were free. Miller's City Band played at the races to enliven the occasion.

"Want to go up to the fairgrounds?" Henry asked Sherwood one Wednesday.

"Nah, I can't," Sherwood said, "Pa plays in the band. I'd catch it if he saw me skipping school."

✳ ✳ ✳

The apple harvest was a large one and O.M. Mallernee was in the market. He was working with Queen Fruit Dryers and was asking farmers to bring bushels of apples to him.

"I'll pay the highest market price," he said, "Bring samples so we can agree upon the price before you haul it here." He wanted to cover all bases so there would be no dissatisfaction.

By September 10th, Mallernee dry house was in full blast with large forces of men, women and boys at work. The dried apples were of fine appearance, blanched and white. Many of the boys of Clyde including Karl and Sherwood worked at Mallernee's, dumping apples into bins, sorting out the unusable apples, packaging the finished product. They collected pocket change and had plans for their ready cash.

On the last day of September, the dry house was shut down for repairs. Mr. Mallernee was increasing the capacity of the drying apparatus so that nearly 200 bushels more apples per day could be taken care of.

Other businesses requiring apples were thriving. David Wise was busy with his sorghum, jelly, and apple butter business, and he had put out a request for sweet apples of mild flavor. His cider mill was at the old vinegar factory on Church Street near McPherson Cemetery.

Sherwood and Karl spent happy days on Mechanic Street and the West Cherry, Spring Avenue area. Sherwood, Herman and their chums met in the cave on Spring Avenue. Herman had shown Sherwood the cave when they first became acquainted and the Andersons lived out on South Main.

It was a natural type cave in the ridge along the bank bluff along Sucker Run. A large rock jutted out at the opening of the cave. The cave had only a small opening and to allow all the members inside, the boys scraped and dug dirt out of the inside of the cave.

Sherwood, who by this time was a voracious reader, read everything he could find, had read and become familiar with Mark Twain's *Tom Sawyer*. The boys met in

the cave to discuss hair-raising plans of theft and piracy.

"Everyone signs in blood on the rock," Sherwood said, "First name only, so we can't be traced."

"Why?" one of the boys asked.

"Because," Sherwood said, "Everyone swears in blood. When you sign in blood, you become a real member of the gang."

By now, Sherwood had become the natural leader of the gang. So he was quite upset when the Major announced the annual move to another house.

"This is the best place we've ever lived! All my friends are here," Sherwood said.

Karl and Irve were sad. They'd be leaving Henry and Willie next door, going to who knows what?

Adventures with Spondulkies

In the early days of Clyde, in the 1820s one of the settlers, Samuel MacMillen built a log cabin at the top of the hill at Race Street and West Maple. The early Methodist settlers worshipped at MacMillen's cabin before they built their church. MacMillen was strict; absolutely no work was done on Sunday. The hill became known as "Piety Hill."

Raccoon Creek ran parallel to Race Street, past the fairgrounds property where it drained into Waterworks Pond. It spilled over the dam and meandered north under bridges on South Street, Buckeye and Maple Streets, all the way to Sandusky Bay.

Maple Street ran in a southwesterly direction from Main Street on out into the country. Race Street joined West Maple at the top of the hill at Ezra Hall's greenhouse, ran south, crossing South Street, Manhattan, Prospect, and Liberty.

All of this area was called Piety Hill. Beyond Piety Hill was farmland. Within Piety Hill were orchards, gardens and nurseries, and a community of citizens.

This time, the Andersons moved to Piety Hill on Race Street, several doors from South Street. The backyard sloped down to Waterworks Pond, and a diagonal path led southeast to the fairgrounds.

The house resembled a child's drawing: a gable front with a door in the center and a window on each side of the door and a porch across the front. It was a one story with a large attic where the boys would sleep.

Sherwood made friends with one boy about his age. Jimmy Moore lived down on the east side of Race Street near the corporation line. His father was a Captain in Company F of the Ohio 72nd. He'd been captured and taken prisoner at the Battle of Brice's Cross Roads in Mississippi, was released and served in the army until the end of his term.

He wasn't well. Jimmy's mother, Mary Jane, was much younger and she took care of her ailing husband. They had two children, Blanche and Jimmy. Jimmy was left to his own devices a good part of the time.

Sherwood and Jimmy explored the area of Coon Creek toward the end of Race Street near where Jimmy lived. There was a spot, a little hidden valley where the creek narrowed and meandered through a long grassy bank. It was secluded with low hanging vines and trees.

"This will be our secret spot," the boys pledged to each other. When things get tough, we can escape to this place."

The boys shook hands solemnly to seal the pact.

❈ ❈ ❈

Just before Christmas, Irve Anderson's school friend, Irving Clapp, known as "Turkey" was playing with another classmate, Gene Drown over at Turkey's place. The two boys were amusing themselves by melting lead and molding bullets. In some unknown way, after the lead had been poured into the mold, it exploded, sending hot lead into Gene's face, burning his right eye andd cheek badly. Turkey escaped with slight burns.

The Major and Robert Clapp, Turkey's father were acquainted. Robert was a retired farmer and the Clapps lived out on the corner of Maple and Walnut.

"You just never know what these youngsters will get into," Bob Clapp said to the Major.

The Major agreed. "Every day is an adventure," he said. "It could have been much worse."

❋ ❋ ❋

There was a school entertainment Thursday and Friday, December 16 & 17, 1886. Adults paid an admission fee of fifteen cents. Tickets were sold at Huntley's Jewelry Store. The younger students performed on Thursday evening.

Herman Hurd recited, "Go On." Johnnie Botsford's recitation was titled, "Opinions of Grandmothers." Harry Heffner offered, "I Will Never Drink." Willie Sargeant sang, "Nobody Asked You To." Sherwood's recitation was titled, "The Woodpecker."

Mabel Supner sang a little ditty, "The Dollie's Fate." Four little girls, including Jennie Baker presented a dialogue. Jennie Bemis offered a piano solo.

The bird-like voices and childish prattle of the recitations always appealed to the older audience members.

On Friday evening the older students, Karl and Stella Anderson, Cliff Paden, Willie Wilder and others recited.

❋ ❋ ❋

In April 1887 the excitement around town was the promise of the gas well. Cities and towns across Northwestern Ohio prepared for a gas boom. Wagons from Toledo hauled cans of nitroglycerin to Tiffin, Fremont, Findlay, Fostoria and Gibsonburg, as well as Clyde, for drilling the wells.

A well was dug in Clyde near Ames Woods. A Findlay man who came to torpedo it said he never saw better indications in a well before it was shot. The gas had been confined to an inch pipe, extended outside the derrick. When lighted, it should shoot out a flame a distance of twenty feet or more and should be a boomer when properly shot, he said.

Sherwood, Herman, Willie Sargeant, Johnnie Botsford and other boys of the town watched the operations from a distance. The danger, the furious preparations, the 'Stay back!' 'Keep away', commands excited the boys and they covered their heads and ears to ward off the explosions.

And there were explosions, but nothing except mud and dirt and water. The boys watched for months.

One day there was a bit of excitement.

"Wow!" The boys felt it. In fact everyone else did too. The explosion shook every house in town and the boom was heard five miles away. But it was not a gusher. It was not even a well being shot. A couple of empty nitroglycerin cans had been taken to Ames Woods, near the gas well and exploded.

A big well was struck at Tiffin. Also the first gas well drilled by the city of Fostoria was said to be a boomer and equal to any of the Findlay wells. At Huron, while drilling for water, the drillers struck a good vein of gas at a depth of 110 feet. The flame burned ten feet high.

The only luck Clyde had was bad. Finally the drillers struck a vein, but it was a weak one. Soon after, some dastards set the gas on fire. They turned the pipe so that the flame burned the derrick. McPherson Hook and Ladder went to the scene to extinguish the fire. One leg of the derrick had burned off.

The damage was not repaired and the high winds shortly afterward, blew the derrick over on its side. The boys went out to Ames Woods to view the damage.

"If that isn't a sad sight," one of the boys said.

The derrick lay prostrate.

"Like a fallen soldier," another said.

Adventures with Spondulkies **37**

By the end of May 1887, classes for the school term were over. Summer loomed ahead with the promise of wonderful adventures for the Anderson brothers, Herman Hurd, Cliff Paden and Henry Bardshar.

"Fred's home from the army for a while," Cliff announced. "He's a sergeant now."

Cliff was relating the events to the others as they played cards up in Henry's barn on Mechanic Street. The rain fell gently on the rusted machinery in the Bardshar's back yard.

Cliff continued, "Fred had to carry some election returns to Toledo for Company I. Colonel Norton resigned and they voted in Colonel Keyes. Anyhow Fred was the one to do the traveling. You'd have thought he was going to a foreign country. Mom carries on when anyone leaves."

"Probably all that fuss when they come home too," Karl said.

"That too," Cliff said. "Ma packed up Carrie and Miss Scott and sent them off to visit my Aunt Frankie in Berlin Heights. What a to-do."

"Miss Scott, the principal?" one of the boys asked.

"She's different when she's away from school. Actually, she's sort of family."

"Hah!" one said, "Like Old Man Ginn would be like family."

Cliff went on. "When they get back, Miss Scott will go to Van Wert for the summer. That's where she's from."

The boys continued their chatter. Karl mentioned the party the Eugene Mathews had for their daughter, Pearl, at their house on Piety Hill.

"Hanging lanterns and fiddle music and the works over at the Mathews," Karl said.

"The night after commencement was the alumni banquet," Henry said. "It's a big doings. Mary and Fronie both went."

Commencement was on June 9th, a Thursday at Terry's Hall. There were parties all over town for the seven young ladies who graduated. The evening following graduation was the Alumni Banquet and the new class of graduates was welcomed into the society. Henry related the activities as told to him by his sisters.

"There were speeches and songs and toasts, not to mention all the feasting. Mary said Fronie responded to a toast and proclaimed, 'To F.M. Ginn, the educational godfather of us all.'"

Cliff clutched his stomach. "Oh, I think I'm going to be sick."

The others laughed at Cliff's antics. They continued the card playing and the rain fell softly.

"So Fronie's home for the summer?" one of the boys asked.

"Fronie resigned from being Port Clinton principal," Henry answered. "Says she's not going back next year."

"They didn't fire her, did they?" Karl asked.

"No," Henry answered. "She quit. Says she can make more money other places."

"Where?" the boys all questioned. The idea of making more money was intriguing to them.

"Out West," Henry said. "Mary's back from Nebraska and I know the girls have been talking about going back.

It's going to kill Ma. It was bad enough when Fronie went to Port Clinton." Henry paused. "Nellie's out west in Kansas and Eddie and Otis are out there somewhere."

"My cousin, Frank Lay is in Georgia," Cliff said. "Uncle Hark is superintendent for some lumber business down in Darien, Georgia."

"Did Frank go by himself?" Karl asked.

Frank Lay was sixteen. His sister, Bessie was younger. He left just before school was out.

"He went by himself, but actually, Seba Wickwire and his son, Scott were going to Florida and left on the same train. Had to change trains in Cincinnati, took the Queen and Crescent Route from there."

"That's an adventure," one of the boys said, "Goodbye teachers. Goodbye schoolbooks. I'm heading South."

"Actually, it was, 'Goodbye Virgil, goodbye Latin'," Cliff said.

The boys were silent, each with his thoughts. The rain pattered on the tin roof of the old barn while the boys shuffled and dealt out cards.

"Won't be long now," Henry said, "Till I'm out West too.

❊ ❊ ❊

In the summer of 1887 the youngsters of the town enjoyed their freedom. There were those who had regular chores to do and those who seemed to be running small businesses.

Cliff Paden was a regular businessman, listed in the Clyde Directory as a newsboy. His brother, Fred, now back in town was a Western Union Telegraph employee. Harry Rhodes, who lived across the street from the Padens substituted for him.

The Major thought Karl should learn a trade. John Ervin at the harness shop took Karl in as his only apprentice. Karl covered the walls of the harness shop with pictures. He drew directly on the walls with pieces of charcoal he picked out of the wood fire ashes. He drew on sheets of paper John brought from the butcher shop. John would point out his favorite drawings to the customers. "Son," he'd say to Karl, "Where's that picture of Ma's cat you did yesterday?"

"I wasn't quite satisfied." Karl answered, "I'm still working on it."

"Well, you've got yourself a fine artist," the customer would compliment John. Karl never corrected John Ervin. He allowed strangers to believe he was John's son.

Karl saw quite a bit of Henry Bardshar and together they planned money-making schemes, which never seemed to pan out.

Sherwood flitted from here to there, the cave on Spring Avenue with Herman Hurd, helping Cliff at the depot.

Karl and Sherwood both tended their garden. The rabbits got their early lettuce, worms took care of the radishes, the beans wilted in the sun and the corn was not knee-high.

"Let's hope we have a few tomatoes," Sherwood said.

The weather was hot that July. Besides traveling into town to spend time with his classmates, Sherwood went to visit Jimmie Moore.

They crept through the corn rows, through the fields and underbrush to their secret hideaway. Wild grapes had grown up around the trees and the vines hung down. Sherwood and Jimmie stripped off their clothes, hung them on branches and swung naked from the vines. Giving whoops and screeches, the boys played they were jungle monkeys. They waded and splashed in the cool water, then lay naked on the grassy bank of the creek. It was still and all they could hear was the rustling of the leaves and the lapping of the water. Raccoons came out of the brush to eat berries.

Sherwood and Jimmie played down in their secluded niche through the summer. Whenever Sherwood wanted a quiet place by himself, he'd head for that secret place.

❋ ❋ ❋

Although the Major had a drink or two at any number of saloons around town, he was a frequent customer of Charley Shuter's.

At a meeting in late May 1887 Clyde Council decided to put a prohibition resolution on the ballot. As a result of the resolution, several of the saloon fronts were painted black. One of the villagers said, "It's probably a sign of mourning over the prospective closing ordinance."

Cliff Paden's cousin, Frank Crockett and Frank's friends were concerned about the closing of the saloons and discussed the issues among themselves. They decided to hold a mock election. They used tickets like the voters at the regular polls and had a judge and clerks. The mock election was held on Monday, June 20th at Frank Crockett's on South Main Street. Ninety-four boys between the ages of ten and twenty-one took part. Ninety votes were to close the saloons and four were against it.

One of the old-timers of the village commented, "If that is an index to the way the boys will vote when they are of age, the saloons may well look to their interests."

In July the Enterprise was favoring the Dow Law and several saloon owners boycotted the newspaper. Ben Jackson, the editor, named them and stated: "We beg to inform them and the people of Clyde generally that we shall endeavor to get out the paper as usual, or at least a few weeks more – long enough, in fact to see that the saloons are driven from town."

There were those townspeople called, 'rowdies' or 'toughs.' They were picked up, from time to time, by Marshal Letson. Then there was an appearance before Mayor Paden.

Smoky Pete was in Tiffin last week and was unable to keep sober. He was 'run in' for drunkenness, but was released and ordered to leave town.

"He got." Cliff related the story to Karl and Sherwood. "Smoky Pete is always in trouble. He's out of jail just now, I guess, but last week he really created a disturbance at Mrs. H. Baker's bakery."

"Drunk again," Karl stated.

"Drunk as a skunk," Cliff said. "The marshal filed the complaint and Smoky Pete was sentenced to clean-up and white-wash Brown's Hotel.

The boys laughed.

"You know he did a good job in remarkably good time. The marshal let him go. Who knows how long he'll be sober?"

"What's Smoky Pete do?" Sherwood asked, "Does he have a regular job?"

Sherwood was always curious about other people's lives.

"He's a wood sawyer and he does odd jobs," Cliff said. "He pitches in wherever he's needed. He helped move the heavy equipment at the Enterprise when they changed locations." Cliff went on, "Pa says he's a great reader of newspapers. He's up on current affairs and can talk on any subject. When he's sober, he's quiet and industrious, but when he's drunk, look out. He's a terror."

"I guess so," Karl said.

Cliff went on. He was enjoying telling the boys all the information he had picked up.

"Pa says if something comes up when he's in jail and he needs to leave on his parole of honor, he keeps his word and returns. Pa says he's a queer compound of a man."

"Sounds like your Pa is right," Karl said.

"My Pa is hoping they get this business about the saloon closings taken care of. Too many mean drunks loose around town," Cliff said.

"Drunks aren't always mean." Sherwood said. "Sometimes they're happy."

Cliff shook his head as if to say, 'I've never seen a happy drunk.'

Sherwood and Karl too, were thinking about their father. He had never been picked up for drinking that they were aware of. They knew he had been drunk because they'd listened to their mother reprimand him. But he sang and whistled and told them bedtime stories and danced jigs when he'd had lots to drink. They hadn't seen him vile, or angry, or mean. Stubborn, maybe, but not mean.

* * *

At ten o'clock on the Friday morning of July 29, 1887, all citizens of Clyde who were not occupied in the fields or engaged in services or shop keeping lined Main Street for a parade.

Jeakles Wonderful Roman Hippodrome Races had come to town. The procession made its way through the village to the fairgrounds on South Main. Fifteen ponies imported from East India wore rich Russian harness with chimes of bells in silver trimmings, plumes and tassels. The diminutive horses were driven four abreast to miniature chariots.

All children under twelve were admitted to the races free. Sherwood wouldn't be eleven until September. Karl hadn't made up his mind to spend his money to go or not.

"I will definitely not miss this," Sherwood said. He was a boy about town and even when he did have to pay, he said he'd figure a way to get a free pass.

The first event on the program was a four-abreast Pony Hippodrome Race, best two in three, half-mile dash. There were other trotting, pacing, running and special races.

Sherwood leaned over the fence to watch the horses run. He loved the racetrack. Sometimes he cut through the backyards on Piety Hill, jumped the creek and trudged up the hill to the fairgrounds. He had a vivid imagination and pretended he was a race driver. He roamed around the vacant fairgrounds by himself, sometimes with Henry Bardshar, sometimes with Irve and sometimes with Herman Hurd, but mostly alone.

✱ ✱ ✱

Karl, Sherwood, Cliff and Henry were all gathered in Bardshar's barn one early fall day. The annual Clyde Fair Premium list was printed and the boys were discussing it.

"Easy way to make some Spondulkies, Henry said, "Just enter your stuff and collect your prizes."

"Like what?" Sherwood asked.

"You got a garden," Henry said, "Look here." He pointed to the list. "A prize for the tallest corn stalk."

"That lets us out," Sherwood said, "Largest hen's egg lets you in, Henry."

Henry laughed. "Think I'll enter the whole chicken and skip the egg."

"You ought to enter some drawings, Karl," Cliff said, "You're better than my cousin Mayme Almond. I know she'll enter."

"I'll think about it," Karl said.

"I'm gonna enter my boat," Henry said.

"What boat?" the boys chorused.

"Just a little boat I made, whittled, carved, glued together, painted up in my workshop." Henry was full of surprises. "Enter some stuff from your garden," he said to the Anderson brothers.

"Hah!" they both laughed.

The boys' garden was a disaster. They salvaged what did grow and tried to peddle onions and tomatoes door-to-door, but the homeowners had better vegetables from their own gardens.

"I'm gonna enter my turnip beets," Henry said.

"Anything else, Henry?"

"Yeah," Henry said, "My tufted toilet cushion."

"What?" the boys asked.

"Don't laugh," Henry said, "It's pretty good. My sisters taught me. I made it for Ma."

❋ ❋ ❋

The annual Clyde Fair opened on Tuesday, October 11th, 1887, and ran for four days. The main feature was harness racing. Clyde was becoming celebrated for fast horses. Some owners had horses for sale. B.F. Heffner, the auctioneer, was one who was offering a yearling colt at a reasonable price.

On the last day of the Fair there were a couple of special races. Trotting a mile in the nearest to five minutes for a silver cup. A, Heter of Bellevue was the winner. "Prince," owned by George Supner of Clyde won a whalebone whip. The prize was for trotting nearest to four minutes. Supner, who owned several horses, was

also a dealer in furniture and displayed a set of bedroom furniture in Floral Hall.

Floral Hall was completely filled with a brilliant display of fancy work and works of art of all kinds along with commercial displays. There were displays of laces, embroidery, crocheted and knitted items and drawings, paintings and some crafts.

Displays of the best of fruits, grains, and vegetables were featured. G.W. Welker's sewing machines and musical instrument display was a feature of Floral Hall. Others showing wares were Hunter Tool and William Gillett & Sons with their boots and shoes. The stock stalls were so full that some of the horses had to be sheltered downtown. Carriages, carriage goods, reapers, and mowers were on exhibition. A number of them sold.

There were activities with prizes for young and old. The marshal and his crew were on hand to keep order and they did. Mothers felt safe letting their children go to the fair. They were cautioned, however, against talking to strangers. Pickpockets and swindlers were at every gathering, no matter how small or large. Merchants offered special sales during the fair and geared up for the long lean winter months.

It was an exhilarating time with fall in the air. There was the warm, mellow smell of apples and cider, before the crisp cool days with frost.

The Andersons attended the fair. Sherwood hung over the fences, watched the trotters run, talked to anyone who was ready to talk, or listen. Karl went back again and again to Floral Hall to examine and marvel at the art displays

The boys, Karl, Sherwood, Cliff, Herman Hurd, Willie Wilder and a few others clustered around Henry Bardshar. They clapped him on the back and offered congratulations. He had won ribbons on his turnip beets, his Plymouth Rock hens, his miniature boat, and his tufted toilet seat.

He was modest. "I just wanted to get some Spondulkies. I'm saving up. You won't see me next year at the fair. I'll be out in the far west dealing with the Indians."

Cliff was reassuring Karl. "Do you see what I mean, Karl? My cousin Mayme won seventy-five cents on her pencil drawing. You can do better."

Karl listened quietly. Cliff went on. "Even my Aunt Tine Lay got seventy-five cents for her crazy-work quilt. You should try next year."

"I'll think about it," Karl said. He didn't mention to Cliff or the others that it cost money to enter and he didn't have it.

❋ ❋ ❋

There was an old saying in Clyde, 'If you dip your feet in Coon Creek and move away, you will return.' And many did. There were those people who vowed to leave

Clyde and never return. Whether it was a domestic situation, gambling debt gone wrong, a lover's quarrel, or a political problem, sooner or later those people returned. The Andersons vowed to stay in Clyde, but not necessarily in the same house.

By the fall of 1887, the Andersons had moved again.

The yellow house, a two-story frame dwelling sat on the edge of an embankment. At the rear was a small barn and a high wooden fence. There was a large beech tree and an old Indian spring at the base. A barrel had been sunk in the ground and was the source of drinking water for the neighboring families. A lid was kept on the barrel for safety. A little bridge crossed over Sucker Run and the stream meandered around, crossing Mechanic Street and running into Raccoon Creek.

Sherwood was ecstatic. The Indian cave where Sherwood, Herman Hurd, and the others signed their names in blood was in the Anderson's back yard,

The move to Spring Avenue pleased Karl almost as much as Sherwood. Karl didn't care anything about the cave, or the secret society. When he wanted adventure, he sought out Henry Bardshar. Henry was always involved in some scheme to make money to get a good 'stash' and go out West. Now, Henry was just a hop the fence and cut through a garden and back yard or two to get to Henry's on Mechanic Street. This was much better than the journey from Piety Hill to the Bardshars. So now, Karl could jog over and pick up Henry and go to school.

Herman Hurd was at the end of Spring Avenue at West Cherry, closer for Sherwood, too. And Cliff Paden was in the neighborhood.

The two-story house was fairly new. Darwin Harkness, who was one of the oldest merchants in Clyde, somewhat of a successful Jack-of-all-trades, built the house. He was a cabinet-maker, a store-keeper, a postmaster, and a partner in the Clyde Banking Association. He had two identical houses constructed on Spring Avenue and later he built a row of five houses on the opposite side of the street. Some were brick and some were frame. This was good rental property for Darwin Harkness.

Emma arranged and rearranged the pieces of furniture she had. There was a parlor or sitting room, a dining room and kitchen.

There were more bedrooms than at the Piety Hill house. Stella had her own room. It was larger than Karl's. He had his own room. The other boys were in another and the parents had their own room, of course.

Emma silently went through the routine of preparing yet another house for the coming winter.

"Irwin Anderson," Emma said as the Major came in the door, "This is the fifth time we've moved in as many years. I refuse to move one more time!"

❋ ❋ ❋

When Sherwood felt he needed to be alone, he would head out to the end of Race Street and find the secluded little valley stream where he and Jimmie Moore had their secret hideaway.

Often Sherwood went down to William Miller's Tailor Shop to find a quiet corner to read. Johnny Becker, Miller's apprentice had stacks of reading material and books in the shop. He read Mark Twain's *Tom Sawyer* and James Fenimore Cooper's *The Last of the Mohicans* down there. Sherwood's concentration was so intense, Herman often had to shake him to get his attention.

The books gave him an idea. He formed a small play-acting role for brother Irve as Uncus, the Indian and himself, as Hawkeye, the scout. The two of them staged Wild West shows for the train passengers at the depot.

They acted out a show-down with wooden knives, then passed the hat for nickels and dimes. The grassy triangle, enclosed with low white picket fence was the perfect stage for the two. They gave a classic finish to their act, Irve crooking his elbow and raising his hand in a 'How' salute, and Sherwood sweeping off his hat with a grand bow. The patrons were more amused than anything with the boys' ingenuity and tossed coins into Sherwood's hat.

The boys of Clyde spent time around the busy depot. Twenty-seven trains ran through town most days, including passenger trains and local freights. The Lake Shore ran eleven. The Wheeling Railroad and the I B & W both ran eight.

One of the locals quipped, "A person can get out of town any time he wants to—almost."

When Irve went off to play with his friend, Turkey Clapp, Sherwood asked Henry Bardshar to take his part.

"Henry, if you are looking to make some money, this is one way to do it," Sherwood said.

"No thanks," Henry said, "I'm not looking for applause and small change. I'm looking for action."

Sherwood looked up Frank McCreery, or Toughy, as he was called. He was an orphan. He didn't go to school. He wore cast-off clothes and scrounged around for food. He slept in Frank Harvey's livery stable. He always needed cash. He told Sherwood he was looking for action but also to make a little money.

Sherwood explained the story and the plan.

"I don't know anything about Uncas and Hawkeye. I want to be a Desparado!."

Sherwood changed the program. They were two Bad Men from the Far West. They carried knives whittled from sticks of wood stuck in their pants and emerged from behind two freight cars by the grain elevator walls.

Toughy cries, "Aha! So it's you, you cur. Now I will taste your heart's blood."

Of course there is a struggle. Knives were drawn and a fight begins. Train passengers stop and watch. Suddenly, Toughy leaps forward and snatches Sherwood's weapon. He has the gleam of a killer. He stabs Sherwood to the heart. Sherwood falls and expires in agony, while Toughy, cap in hand runs among the passengers and collects the nickels and dimes.

"How'd it go with Tough?" Henry asked Sherwood.

"Ma came. No more acting. She said it was too much like begging,"

"Well, you'll think of something else," Henry said.

✳ ✳ ✳

Late one Friday afternoon in the fall of 1887 a merchant in town approached Henry and Karl.

"How'd you fellas like to do a little chore for me?"

"Well, gee, I dunno," Henry dug his toe in the dirt. Karl remained silent. He usually took Henry's lead.

"Tell you what I want you to do," the man said, "I want you to go to Fremont and pick up a horse for me. How's that sound?"

"Well, gee, I dunno." Henry said again. He pushed his hands in his pockets and looked up at the man.

"What do you say, son?" the man asked Karl.

Karl shrugged his shoulders. "Is there gonna be pay for this?"

The man laughed. "So that's it. You want to be paid. Well, I'll give you seventy-five cents. How's that sound?"

"Better," Henry said.

The man pulled the coins out of his pocket, handed them to Henry and they made arrangements for the eight-mile trip. They planned to leave in the morning.

Whenever Karl and Henry got involved in something out of their ordinary routine, Sherwood showed up insisting to take part.

"Aw, let him go, Karl."

They hitched the old roan horse to the buckboard and settled in for the ride to Fremont. It was a dark, cloudy morning with a threat of rain, but the boys' spirits were high and they were ready for adventure. They reached Fremont about noon.

"I am starved," Sherwood said.

"I suppose you're so starved you could eat a horse," Henry answered. With that, the boys laughed hilariously at their humor.

"Chicken dinner. That's what I'd like," Karl said, "A sumptuous, delicious chicken dinner."

"Me too," Henry and Sherwood chorused.

There was a restaurant near their destination and the boys went in. They ordered the chicken dinners as planned and smacked their lips. The bill for the three dinners came to seventy-five cents. Henry produced the coins from his pocket.

"Easy come. Easy go."

They tarried a little over their meal, but following Henry's lead soon were ready to pick up the merchant's horse and be on their way back to Clyde.

Henry tied the frisky white mustang to the back of the buckboard, hopped on the seat and took the reins.

"My turn, Henry," Karl said. "You drove all the way over."

"Fair enough." Henry answered and handed the reins over to Karl.

Sherwood, who usually protested he hadn't had a turn, was content to ride along. Karl kept the old roan to a slow, steady trot. Midway to Clyde, Henry asked Karl to pull over.

"I just want to check the mustang. See if she's tied secure."

Karl nodded and stopped the buckboard. "You tied him, Henry. He ought to be okay."

Sherwood had been watching the proceedings. "Henry, what are you doing? Are you going to ride him?"

"Just going to try him out, that's all." Henry said. He untied the horse, jumped on its back and rode off, motioning for Karl to drive on to Clyde.

A strange transformation came over Henry. He became a whooping Indian. He rode off, then changing direction, came back to the road and the buckboard, then dashed off again. He rode in circles in the fields next to the pike, looping back to lead the buckboard, waving his hat to Karl and Sherwood.

"Sure hope we get the horse back to that man okay, Sherwood." Karl felt responsible. "I should have let him drive."

"Well, you know Henry," Sherwood said, "He'd figure some way to ride that mustang."

Suddenly Henry pulled a revolver out of his trousers belt. He began shooting blanks up in the air.

"Whoa. Whoa, slow down!" Karl yelled. The noise frightened both horses. The roan raced down the pike pulling the buckboard behind it, mud and dirt flying. They ran into the corn shocks, flipped and dumped Karl and Sherwood out.

Henry galloped up to the rig. The roan had got loose and tore around in the field.

"Hey there." One of the farmers coming into town spotted the boys in the field. He hailed the boys, stopped his wagon and came over to help. "Anybody hurt?"

Henry whipped around on the mustang and caught the roan. After a short time the rig was uprighted, the mustang retied to the rear and the boys were on their way.

Henry slouched down, pulled his hat over his eyes. He was quiet for the rest of the trip to Clyde. Karl drove the rig in silence. Sherwood had little to say. They delivered the mustang to the merchant.

"Fine job, boys," the merchant said, "If I need any more horses to get picked up, I'll call on you."

"Sure," Henry said, "We're always glad to help out." The boys waved good-bye and headed toward Mechanic Street.

Would you do it again, Henry?" Karl asked.

"In a minute. Would you?"

"You betcha," Karl said.

"That was a really delicious chicken dinner," Sherwood said.

❋ ❋ ❋

Christmas was approaching and businesses were decked out for the holidays. They offered special bargains. Uptown meat markets had posted notices that they would be closed on Sundays. Alf Pawsey's show window was decorated with all types of footwear. Julius Joseph's store was having a sale. Ladies scarlet underwear at seventy-five cents. The underwear was worth all of $1.25, the sign said.

Sherwood and Herman Hurd sauntered down the street. It was cold but there was no wind. The boys window-shopped along Main Street, looking at the festive displays in the windows. They giggled and poked each other, pulled one another's caps down over their eyes and hooted at the ladies' red underwear.

"Special price, Sherwood," Herman said and laughed, "You could get some for Stella."

"Sure, You could get some for Hattie," Sherwood answered.

They laughed and clapped each other on the shoulders.

Their mouths watered at the Christmas candies and holiday goodies and cakes at the bakeries. All sorts of goods were for sale.

Sherwood looked but didn't buy. The cold of the board sidewalk penetrated through the thin soles of his shoes. He blew on his hands.

"We'd best be getting home," Sherwood said. "Ma will be looking for me."

❋ ❋ ❋

By January 1888 the waterworks reservoir was frozen. Mothers reminded their children of the dangers of the pond and thin ice.

Thin ice was one concern, but another was the barbed-wire that stretched across the upper part of the reservoir and formed an obstruction. Several boys had been badly hurt. One came near losing an eye. A number of skaters appeared around town with jagged scars from the barbed-wire accidents.

Winter Saturdays were filled with chores, but the Anderson brothers found time for skating. Afterwards they looked for their friends in town. Sherwood and Karl, in thin coats and thin-soled shoes, hands jammed in their pockets, made their way up the Mulberry Street hill and down West Buckeye to town. It was a little farther than cutting across Spring and down Cherry Street, but they preferred the walk past the fine houses. B.F. Heffner, the auctioneer, Old Man Ginn and Mrs. Rosaline Bemis, a music teacher were several who lived on that street.

They listened for the sound of the piano as they passed the Bemis house. Familiar tunes, or the rippling practice of scales filled the air. The sounds were fainter during the winter when the house was closed up. In the summer with the doors open, the music filled the George Street end of Buckeye.

Jennie Bemis was a classmate. She was always pleasant and friendly to the brothers. Sometimes, the music was drowned out by the train whistles. The sounds of freight or passenger trains as they screeched to the Clyde station stop. The air hung with coal dust, the acrid smell stinging their nostrils.

Sherwood said he was going down to the tailor shop.

"See if there's anything new to read," Sherwood said. Besides it's warm there."

Karl was on his way to the harness shop.

"Ervin's closed for the day," Sherwood said.

"I know." Karl answered, "I sweep out. The fellows come over."

"Ooooh, ooooh," Sherwood cooed, "And you talk about girrels."

"So what," Karl answered.

❊ ❊ ❊

Usually Karl, Johnny Becker, Willie Wilder, and several others would congregate at the harness shop on a winter's evening. It was warm and smelled of leather. Karl had a stack of either butcher paper or brown wrapping paper saved from parcels at the harness shop. He'd sharpen his pencil with one of the leather knives and draw while the boys talked.

Once in a while Cliff Paden joined them. When he wasn't there, one of the group had a story Cliff had told them.

"I guess it was last Tuesday, outside one of the saloons on Main Street, Shooters, or one of the others," Willie Wilder began. Those gathered looked up. Saloon stories were always interesting.

"There was a big fight. I don't know the fellows personally, myself, but one of the parties is quite a celebrated knocker. His opponent has only one good right arm. We all know who that is."

The boys nodded to each other. "Go on."

"Well, he sent the knocker to the ground in the first round!" The storyteller paused for effect. "He beat him nearly to a pulp. In other words he was woefully marred."

"The one-armed guy beat the knocker up?"

"Yes, he did."

"Cliff told you that? How's he know?"

"According to Cliff, the people who were gathered, separated the two, then the knocker and the one-armed fellow walked together to the mayor's office and prayerfully requested that officer to allow them to pay the five-dollars fine."

"Well, Cliff should know since his Pa's the mayor."

Herman Hurd was out of breath when he caught up with the Anderson brothers and Cliff and Henry.

"Pa's store got robbed!"

Who? What? When?

"Burglars broke the glass in the rear door, reached in and unlocked it. They took a whole lot of knives, a piece of tobacco and a box of cigars."

"Any money? The boys asked.

"No money," Herman answered. "There was money in the safe they could have taken."

"What's the marshal say, Hern?" Sherwood asked.

"Marshal Zan says he believes some young scapegraces committed the robbery. Oh, yes," he added, "He said, 'There is evidently somebody around for whom the yawning penitentiary has no terrors.'"

* * *

Doctor Cyrus Harnden stopped at the harness shop one day in early March. Karl was tacking up one of his drawings on the wall. He had finished sorting small parts into various bins and had little extra time for himself.

Doctor Harnden held out a broken piece of harness to see about getting it repaired. John examined the piece and an agreement was reached.

"I'll have that in working condition tomorrow," John said, "How's the little bride?"

"Umm," Doc Harnden said as he rested his chin on his hand. "She's a bit surprised at what housekeeping is all about." He paused. "I got my own office to run and horse and buggy to keep up, I told her. I can't do it all."

"Well, we all need someone to 'fetch and carry' for us, help us get our own work done," John said.

Doctor Harnden glanced around. He saw the drawings on the wall, but didn't comment on them. His eye fell on Karl.

"You got yourself a helper. Wonder where I could find a helper for my place."

John looked at Karl. He knew Karl wanted to earn as much money as he could.

"Karl Anderson, here, helps me after school. I'd imagine he could stop by your place before school and tend to your chores," John said.

Karl looked up.

"You dependable, son?

Karl stood up. "Yes, sir."

"You afraid of hard work?"

"No, sir," Karl answered, still standing.

"So, Karl, is it?" Karl nodded. "So, Karl, come over tomorrow morning before school. I'll give you your instructions then."

Karl crossed the shop and held out his hand to shake it. The doctor didn't notice. He adjusted his hat.

"I'll be in tomorrow, John, for the harness. I'll see you in the morning, boy," he said in Karl's direction.

❉ ❉ ❉

Citizens of Clyde in the spring of 1888 were talking about the new businesses opening on Main Street.

"It looks as though out town is about to boom!" said one.

"Let 'er boom," came the answer.

Mr. Zack Taylor had leased the Bonam block for five years. When the occupants were moved out he planned to fix it up, add improvements and open a first-class dry goods establishment. Since Mr. Taylor planned to use the entire block, Miss Lina Elliot moved her photograph gallery to another location.

Rumor has it that there was planned a new clothing store, a restaurant, a new boot and shoe store and probably other places of business.

The nurseries of G.S. Pickett and A.B. French were among the busiest places in Clyde. Several carloads a day of choice fruit trees, berry roots and vines had been shipped out. A small army of men had been kept busy at the two nurseries and the proprietors had their hands full in managing and keeping them busy.

Crime in Clyde was not usually a problem. Brown's Hotel had an occupant or two, but they were the regular drunks or a passing vagrant. Burglaries happened once in a while. The April 30 robbery at Hurd's Grocery was one instance. Muggings, hold-ups, and other crimes were unusual. The most serious problem in early May seemed to be horse stealing.

❋ ❋ ❋

The boys of the town gathered around Sherwood. He and Cliff had been down at the depot. There was a cage at the U.S. Express office. They read the label and stepped back. The cage was en route from New York to Huntsville, Ohio and was to be transferred at Clyde.

"What was in the cage, Sherwood?"

After keeping his friends in suspense, Sherwood answered, "Two Blood- Sucking Vampires!"

❋ ❋ ❋

There had been rain on July fourteenth.

"You know the lawyer, Tom Dewey?" Sherwood asked the boys of Clyde.

"Yep." All the boys knew who he was.

"Well, Tom Dewey wants to know why it wouldn't be a good idea for the street committee to buy a few frogs and put them in the mud-holes on Main Street to furnish free music for the town."

The boys laughed hilariously at the suggestion. One commented that for years, Smoky Pete had been after the town to macadamize Main Street.

❋ ❋ ❋

August came hot and dusty.

"Big news, Fellas," Cliff called and joined his companions. "Marshal Zan caught the Hurd Store robber."

"No foolin! Who?"

"Frog Keefe," Cliff said.

The boys were all ears.

"Here's the story, " Cliff explained in his dramatic fashion. "The marshal had been on the lookout for him for a long time. He tracked that affair very closely and found a number of the knives in Fremont where they had been disposed of by Keefe."

"Aha!" the boys nodded.

"But," Cliff continued, "Frog wasn't arrested at that time because of the expense, which the marshal would have been obliged to pay out of his own pocket. But Zan had a good memory and the first time Frog put in an appearance in Clyde, the marshal nabbed him. Pa sent him to jail at Fremont in default of $400 bail."

"Wow!" the boys chorused.

"Yep," Cliff said, "Burglary and larceny."

Growing Up, Moving On

One day in August, 1888 Karl and Cliff were watching the teams of horses and men at work. They were excavating the cellar and preparing to lay the foundation of the Niles Block next to the Farmers and Traders Bank. Mr. H, F. Niles purchased the lot in the early summer. B. F. Heffner's Carriage Repository had been located there but had been moved.

"So what's going up here?" Cliff asked one of the workmen.

"A fine two-story, brick block," the workman answered and turned back to his work.

"My Pa says there are very good prospects that other blocks may go up on Main Street in the near future. He said these are signs of industry and prosperity that every patriotic citizen of the town will rejoice in."

"Well, your Pa knows what's going on in the town," Karl said. "I heard he was real sick and some other person took over as mayor."

"Yeah," Cliff said. "My brother Fred came home from Elmore on account of his illness."

Cliff chuckled a little and Karl gave him a quizzical look.

"Justice George Pruden took over the mayor's job while Pa was sick. He said he wouldn't be mayor for two-hundred dollars a month."

"Why not, for Pete's sake?" Karl asked.

"He said he lost ten pounds, got a lame arm from writing so much, a gathering in his ear, an aggravated case of rheumatism, and a broken heart."
Cliff and Karl both laughed.

"Yep. Pa laughed too, Cliff said, "Pa said George thinks if one little case with Mrs. Burroughs and a few customary complaints from citizens caused all this, a few years experience as mayor would find him in his grave."

Cliff was sober. "Pa laughs about it, but he really isn't well. He's better, but he isn't well."

The boys watched the excavation work in silence for a few minutes. The teams moving dirt and stones piling debris on the wagons, the teams snorting and pawing the ground, straining at their bits as the wagons left the area.

❋ ❋ ❋

Karl and Henry walked on toward school. Karl was deep in thought. Henry was quiet. Finally, Henry broke the silence.

"Karl, I'm going out West."

"I know. You say that almost every day."

"Sure, but this time I mean it. I'm going real soon."

"You're not going to finish school first?"

Henry laughed. "Look at me, Karl. I'm sixteen years old. I'm twice as tall as the kids in my class. Little kids. And they're smart. I been held back so many times."

"Henry, you're not stupid. You don't do the work. You miss school for days."

"Yeah. Well, I can read and I can figure. What else do I need? Do I need History? Philosophy? Latin?"

Karl knew Henry had been wrestling with his school problems for some time.

"Will you write to me, Henry?"

"Probably not. I'll have to write to Ma. That will be enough writing for me."

"I'll go see your mother and get the news from her," Karl said. "Sounds like your mind's made up."

Henry took a deep breath. "Mary's in Holdredge, Nebraska. She's a saleslady. Fronie went out there in August to teach. Otis and Eddie are out West somewhere. Nellie is in Holden, Kansas. I'm going there first. Mac, her husband said I could work with him."

"What's he do?"

"Sells musical instruments."

Karl laughed. Then both of the boys laughed, breaking the tension.

"You were so terrific in music, Henry."

"I know," Henry laughed. "Well, it's a start. It's the gateway to the West. I'm planning on Arizona later. Going to be a miner."

"And fight the Indians," Karl added.

"Yeah. And fight the Indians." They laughed. It was an ongoing joke between the two of them.

The boys were approaching the schoolyard. The bell had rung long ago.

"You go on in, Karl. I'm not going today. I got other things to do."

It was a bright crisp morning. Karl was tempted to go off with Henry.

"Stella will tattle if I'm not there."

❋ ❋ ❋

When Sherwood was about twelve, he took over Karl's position as chore-boy to Doc Harnden. He was up early, out the back door, over the fence and into his duties like a dynamo. He tackled the woodpile, the walks, assorted added tasks with a thoroughness that satisfied the doctor. He was cheerful, with his good

mornings. He gave a tip of his cap, a smile and a good-bye wave as he left.

In the spring and summer the work was pleasant. The air was fragrant with blooming lilacs. Birds sang.

Doctor Harnden usually inspected Sherwood's work from the front porch, sometimes adding an additional task. In warm weather the doctor stood on the top step mopping his brow with a big white handkerchief, his tie unloosened.

On a balmy spring day, Sherwood didn't mind doing small extra jobs or even chatting for a moment.

But in the winter when the doctor ambled out on the porch, his wool muffler snug around his fat neck, fleece-lined gloves warming his hands and heavy galoshes on his feet, Sherwood cringed, hoping the doctor wouldn't delay him.

He felt the frigid sidewalk through his thin-soled shoes. His numb fingers gripped the broom handle as he swept. His cap left his ears exposed and his thin coat was little protection against the raw wind. Sherwood wanted to get finished with the doctor's duties as soon as possible and get moving.

He trotted down to the railroad depot and warmed his hands at the poy-bellied stove. The Cleveland papers were in and ready to be delivered. Clifton Lay Paden was already on the job, untying bundles and counting out papers.

"Hiya, Jobby," Cliff called. How was old Doc this morning? Sober?"

Sherwood waved him off. "He was fine." He was a lot steadier than the Major was this morning, Sherwood thought.

The depot was buzzing. The teletype was clicking. Smoky Pete was sweeping leaves that had blown in back out the door. Train whistles echoed in the distance.

Sherwood gathered up his papers and started down Main Street. He sold morning Cleveland papers to merchants along the way. When he saw an opportunity, he added new customers.

Cliff had an established route. Selling newspapers was his only job. He was the same age as Karl and had been a paperboy since he was eleven.

"You've already got so many jobs, Sherwood. What do you want this one for?"

"Something about selling newspapers, Cliff," Sherwood said, "It's more of a real job. Doc Harnden? That's temporary. When Irve gets older, I'll give Doc Harnden to him. Picking strawberries? That's early summer. You can't pick strawberries in the winter. Same way with setting cabbage."

Sherwood was resourceful. He was an avid reader. He read the front page first and pointed out stories that he thought the villagers would be interested in reading, the latest scandal, or current political happenings and then sell copies to the farmers who came to town to do their shopping.

Sherwood would say, "There's an interesting story in here, all about such and such. I think you'd like to read it. Generally they'd buy a paper. Sherwood sold more papers than any other boy in town.

Trains had pulled in from the East and the West, departed Northward and arrived Southward. Clyde was a busy station with the Lake Shore trains, the Wheeling and Lake Erie Railroad, the Indiana, Bloomington and Western Railway. All day long the whistles blew. Passenger trains and freight trains arrived and departed.

Sherwood watched for the Eastbound trains. He met passengers who boarded or got off. He sold Cleveland papers to those headed east so they'd get the latest hometown news before they got to Cleveland. He used the same routine for the Southern route to Cincinnati.

"Paper, mister? The latest news!" Sherwood's young voice cried out. He had an engaging manner and a ready grin.

One ear was cocked to listen for the school bell. When the first bell rang, Sherwood took care of his final customer of the morning and headed toward school. When he first began his newspaper business he was conscientious about getting to school on time.

He'd race at breakneck speed, hopping over rails and baggage in the freight area, taking his own short cut through back yards of George Street and Maple over to Vine, stubbing his toe, skinning his knee, but arriving seconds before the tardy bell chimed.

As his business prospered and his regular customers chatted, Sherwood sometimes missed hearing the first bell. Since he was going to be late anyway, he took his time arriving.

He was in C Grammar. His teacher was Miss Sarah Suggitt, in her second year of teaching. She watched Sherwood slide into his seat late, nearly every day. She knew about his newspaper route and saw Sherwood as a bright, eager, young lad, interested in getting ahead in the outside world, also trying to do what was expected of him at school. She had a kind, sympathetic heart and helped Sherwood catch up in his studies.

"Come on, Cliff. Lets go," Sherwood called.

"Nah, you go on. I'm going home to see about Pop."

Cliff's attendance record was poor. He was in high school studying Physiology, Physical Geography and Algebra. He managed to make up tests and keep up with the rest of his class. But lately, his father's illness had begun to frighten him.

Henry Paden had been the editor and publisher of the *Clyde Enterprise* for years. When his health failed, he sold the paper.

* * *

Halloween came and went.

"Thankfully," one resident said, "Halloween comes but once a year.

As in other years, the mischief-makers were busy.

Who were the culprits? Toughy McCreery? Willie Sargeant? Moody Dwight? Porch furniture not moved inside was hoisted up on rooftops. Wagons were set up on tops of sheds. Outhouses were overturned.

Some pranksters adorned the front entrance to the People's Bank with paint kegs. They decorated the roof of the Farmer's and Trader's Bank with beer kegs. Last year, the pranksters left beer kegs at church entrances and pastor's residences.

Steps were carried away. Gates were taken off and moved out of sight. Cabbages and turnips were tossed onto porches.

Emma Anderson, as was her usual Halloween custom, added carrots and potatoes to the cabbages and turnips and cooked a pot of stew.

❋ ❋ ❋

Ever since the summer political conventions the town was abuzz with posters and promotions. Clyde was a Republican town supporting Benjamin Harrison. Number of Democrats, the Major included, held out for Grover Cleveland.

Just as they had done since they first knew each other, Herman Hurd and Sherwood took sides. They enjoyed bantering back and forth, mostly imitating their elders.

During election times there was a burst of activity in the town: the campaigns, politicking, hand-shaking, back-slapping and the suppers. There were many of those.

At the harness shop John Ervin said to Karl, "The ladies do not care to talk politics, but do mean to feed their patrons well, make them feel happy, whatever the outcome at the polls.

The lawyer, Thomas P. Dewey, who lived up on the hill at South Main and Arch Street, set up seven boxes of cigars.

"It's a boy! He proclaimed, "Benjamin Harrison Dewey. He howls for the Republicans."

Levi Peck, Henry Bardshar's grandfather, who was 81 years old, announced that he would support Harrison.

"I voted for 'Old Tippecanoe' in 1840 and I'll support his grandson this fall," he said. He had been visiting the Bardshars for several weeks and was on his way back to Huron, Ohio.

Election night there was a ball at the Pythian Armory Hall. The music was by Erastus Gould's orchestra.

"Rat Gould will be in rare form, Emma," the Major announced. "They're going to announce the election returns from the stage."

On Friday, November 9, 1888 the news was definite. Harrison won the election, even though Cleveland had more popular votes. Those who had bets around town collected them.

"Wouldja look at that!" Cliff said as he and Sherwood approached the depot, "in front of the Junction Hotel."

"Empire House," Sherwood corrected him," "It's a fruit stand."

The boys went over to examine it. They were at the station early to collect their papers from the train.

"Oh, I heard about this," Cliff said. "Frank Welker won the bet. He gets to keep Willie Thorpe's fruit stand."

Sherwood knew the Welkers. He delivered papers to the hotel. They had settled in the town in September, 1887, took over the Junction Hotel, changed the name, spruced the place up, sodded the yard, put in walks. He had even moved his seventy-five year old mother from Hicksville, so he could take better care of her.

"He's the only Republican saloon-keeper in Clyde, and Pa says he's too nice a fellow to be in the saloon business," Cliff said to Sherwood.

Sherwood said, "I don't see him much, only her, Mrs. Julia. She's usually in the kitchen and she pays me for the paper."

"The fruit stand is, or was, Willie Thorpe's. Those two made a bet. Welker would give Willie his hotel if Cleveland won, and Willie would give Frank the fruit stand if Harrison won," Cliff said. "Well, you know the results."

The two boys were untying and sorting their papers, working hurriedly to get finished before the first bell.

The fruit stand stayed in front of the Empire House for several days. Willie saw Frank and said he wanted to rent the stand. Frank said he could have it for fifty cents a month. Then just as Willie was about to leave, Frank pulled a five-dollar bill from his pocket.

"This is for paying your debt so promptly," Frank said.

"Frank Welker's usually a nice guy," Cliff said to Sherwood, "He's interested in everything in town from sports to politics, Pa says, but he's got a temper and it always lands him in trouble."

❋ ❋ ❋

There was a snowstorm on Monday, November 26. The ground snow lingered. When Sherwood came home and stomped into the house on Thursday, Emma reprimanded him.

"Sorry," he mumbled, and went on with his adventure of the day.

"Down at the depot..." This was the usual start of one of his experiences. "There was a big box. It was transferred at Clyde, going from Elmira, New York to Indianapolis, Indiana."

The Anderson children, also Emma and the Major looked up. Sherwood went on.

"On the box was written, 'Benjamin: as you captured me in New York, I am coming home to roost.' The box was going to next-President Benjamin Harrison," Sherwood said.

"Go on. What was in the box?" Irve asked impatiently.

"It was a monster bird, a big American Eagle," Sherwood said.

There was the usual reaction from the Anderson family, and Sherwood explained. "Agent Hess says all sorts of goods are going by express to the next President Harrison."

"Humph," the Major said, "Cleveland would have been a better choice.

※ ※ ※

May 28, 1889, a Tuesday evening at Terry's Opera House, the pupils of Professor Griffith and Miss Zella Brigham were giving a program. It was to raise money to purchase books for the school library. Cliff Paden was repeating his declamation entitled, "How Congress Fought for Sheridan."

"No, I'm not going to pay to go hear Cliff recite. I hear him every day." Sherwood said. "Fifteen cents. I can get three dishes of ice cream for that."

Sherwood and Herman Hurd discussed the program.

"Cliff's family will all go. And his cousins. They'll fill up the hall."

Professor Griffith introduced Clifton Paden. The audience gave him a warm welcome. Cliff came to the center of the stage and bowed. He was a handsome lad, with deep-set eyes, a cleft chin and a jutting jaw. He was tall, with a shock of wavy brown hair. In his suit and tie and regal bearing, he looked older than his fifteen years.

He recited his declaration flawlessly and at the conclusion, the rafters rang with the resounding applause. The audience gave him a standing ovation.

"Your father would have been so proud," one from the audience said to him.

Henry Paden had died March 1, 1889.

❈ ❈ ❈

Karl was fifteen the summer of 1889, and it was the first summer without his pal, Henry Bardshar.

"What good times we had," Karl thought. "Wonder what Henry is doing now. Maybe I'll go see his Ma. See if she's heard anything." Karl was lost in thought as he walked down the village street.

"Hello, there," a voice called.

"Hello," Karl answered.

It was Frank Hadley Ginn. He was leading a white pointer dog.

"It's been a long time." He stopped to talk. "My father tells me you Anderson boys are the ones to see if there are any chores to be done. 'Jobby.' Isn't that what they call your brother?"

"Yes, it is." Karl said. A rather uncertain smile twisted at the corner of his mouth. "Sherwood is a real go-getter."

"What I had in mind was some help from you. It's a paying job. My partner here, is going to have his portrait painted this afternoon. I need someone to hold him still." He gave his dog a friendly pat.

"Sounds interesting," Karl said. "I'm not busy. I can help you out." Karl reached down and petted the dog. "I like dogs."

They made arrangements to meet at John B. Tichenor's Art Studio in the Niles Block on Main Street.

At the studio the three talked about the future. Hal Ginn planned to be a lawyer. He asked Karl what he planned to do. Karl shrugged.

"Put it this way, Karl," Hal said, "What would you rather do than anything else?"

"Hah! That's easy. I'd just draw and paint all day."

"I thought so," J. B. said, "A fellow artist. John Ervin has shown me your drawings."

"He's shown them to everybody he can." Karl said.

It was getting late in the afternoon and they decided to call it a day. Hal wanted to get his dog outside for some exercise.

"I've just background and some finishing touches, Hal. Stop by in a couple of days," J.B. said. "Karl, I want to talk to you a minute before you go."

"Sure," Karl said. He pitched in and helped J.B. with the cleanup. Hal's dog was pulling at his leash, ready to go. Hal pulled his wallet from his pocket and handed Karl a bill.

"Oh, no!" Karl said, "I can't take that."

"I told you it was a paying job and you handled it well. J.B. will get paid handsomely for his work. He knows it and he won't refuse the pay."

"He's right, Karl," Tichenor said. "I might charge him double, seeing how fond he is of that old hunting dog."

Hal gave a smile and a wave and left the studio.

J.B. Tichenor motioned for Karl to sit down. He told Karl he had been planning to have classes now that he had moved to the Niles Block.

"I've been here since March, Karl, and look at this mess. I can't seem to get caught up enough to sweep the floor."

Karl listened intently, nodding and understanding. J.B. went on.

"How's your feeling about Sunday, Karl? I mean- do you go to church?"

"Hah!" Karl laughed. "Only if I can't get out of it."

"Then you wouldn't mind working for me on Sunday?"

"I wouldn't mind at all." Karl answered.

J.B. knew Karl still worked at the harness shop before and after school and through the summer.

"What I had in mind was a trade-off. You come in Sunday and clean my studio and I'll give you art lessons."

"It's a deal," Karl said. He didn't need to think about it.

❋ ❋ ❋

One late August day before school started, Sherwood, Herman, and other friends of theirs were playing in the back yard of the Hurd's home on West Cherry Street.

Jimmie Moore, who now lived on West Forest Street behind the Hurd's was playing by himself. He was an adventurous boy. Several years ago, he and Sherwood swung like monkeys along Raccoon Creek. Jimmie had a small Flobert rifle. He may have been pretending he was a frontiersman and the boys at the Hurds were Indians. No one knows.

Thoughtlessly, even though Jimmie was eleven, he pointed the weapon towards the Hurd residence and fired. Maybe he thought they'd join in, take cover, and pretend to return fire.

Instead, the ball from the rifle struck Herman in the eye.

Herman screamed. Jimmie fled. Jimmie was sure he was in trouble.

"Run! Go get his Pa!" Sherwood yelled to one of the others.

Herman winced in pain. "I'm gonna be blind, Jobby!" Herman said between gasps of pain.

"Nah," Sherwood said, comforting his friend, "Your Pa will get you to a doctor."

Others had gathered around with cries of "What happened?" and "Oh, my, is he all right?" Herman's eye became suffused with blood. They believed the bullet had penetrated the eye.

"T. P. Hurd arrived on the scene in record time and at once took Herman to Cleveland on the next train.

In Cleveland, T. P. Hurd took his son to the eminent oculist, Dr. D. B. Smith. It was thought at first a very serious wound. Dr. Smith examined Herman's eye and ascertained that the ball had not entered the eye.

"A close call," Dr. Smith said. He prescribed treatment. "Prospects for an entire recovery are quite good," he said.

After Herman got home, the neighborhood boys all came to see him except Jimmie Moore.

Herman's eye was bandaged so that he wouldn't strain it and so that it would have a chance to heal.

"Too bad your bandage isn't black," Sherwood said. "You'd look like a pirate."

School opened on Monday, September 2, 1889 with 468 pupils enrolled. There was an increase over last year. Teachers greeted students. The Pledge of Allegiance was recited. Class assignments were made. Rules were set and school was dismissed. It was Labor Day and a holiday.

Herman wore his eye patch like a banner. Anyone who had not heard of the incident knew about it now. Jimmie Moore was pointed out as the culprit.

❋ ❋ ❋

The opening day of the Clyde Fair was Tuesday, September 24th. Schools were closed so the students could attend. J.W. Robinson set up his lunchroom not too far from the racetrack. Each year the Fair Committee and the promoters promised a larger and better fair.

Sherwood and Herman Hurd prowled the grounds watching races and special events. Sherwood was mindful of the time, listening for train whistles. He was a businessman and whether there was a fair or not, he still had to take care of his papers.

"Look at that, Hern," Sherwood said, "Some kind of a fakir?"

The boys were watching the operator of a machine. He poured a pound of sugar into the machine, added a few drops of red coloring and started it up.

"Look at it go!" Herman said.

The machine whirled rapidly. A cloud of pink frothy candy spun out of the machine. The operator caught it in paper bags.

"Looks delicious," Herman said.

"We'll take a bagful," Sherwood said to the proprietor and fished in his pocket for the coins. Sherwood was full of questions. "How does it work?" he asked the proprietor. "How much of this spun candy does a pound of sugar make?"

"About a bushel," the operator said.

Sherwood thanked him and the boys wandered off with their treat. Herman dipped into the bag and stuffed a handful of the spun sugar in his mouth.

"It's nothing!" he said, "It melts into nothing!"

Sherwood pulled a cluster of the pink foam out of the bag and stuck it in his mouth.

"You're right, Hern," Sherwood said, "It's nothing. Sweet, but nothing." He paused, squinted his eyes, cocked his head. "How many of these bags would you say were in a bushel, Hern?"

"Oh, I dunno. Twenty? Twenty-five?"

"Tisn't a very big bag." Sherwood said, "The old fakir is getting rich. A pound of sugar and he gets all this profit. You know what a pound of sugar costs at your Pa's store."

Sherwood mentally counted up what the proceeds amounted to. Since he'd been a newspaper boy and bought and sold papers he could do sums fast in his head.

"Jobby, don't forget. He's got to pay for the gasoline that runs the engine. He probably barely breaks even."

Whose side are you on?" Sherwood asked, "He's a fakir. Leave it at that."

❋ ❋ ❋

On Thursday, September 26, the boys of Clyde and their families watched the balloon ascension at the Fairground. People came from miles around to the Clyde Fair. No parachute leaping had ever before been attempted in the county.

Professor R.J. Hawkins, the celebrated Cleveland aeronaut was the headliner. The crowd was thick as people gathered together to watch the professor lift off in his balloon. He waved a white silk handkerchief to the crowd and smiled broadly as the balloon lifted off from the ground. A roar of applause accompanied his take-off. The balloon rose swiftly but moments into the flight the professor encountered a current of air, which prevented him from ascending as high as he intended.

He leaped from the balloon and made the jump successfully. His parachute landed safely in Mr. Mack's orchard, just east of the fairgrounds, less than a half-mile from the starting point. The balloon collapsed and came down near Birdseye's Corners, two miles away.

On Friday, the boys of Clyde watched the preparations of Miss May LaZelle. Miss LaZelle was the only lady living who had accomplished the daring feat of parachute descents. So far this season she had made a hundred balloon ascensions and eight parachute drops.

Her balloon ascended considerably higher than the Professor's had the day before. She cut loose from the balloon at a height of nearly a mile and made a very successful landing not far from the spot where the Professor came down yesterday.

There was a gasp from the crowd and 'Oh's' and Ah's as she floated down. The young and old of Clyde attended: the Andersons, the Hurds, Willie Sargeant's family, Johnnie Botsford and all the others were there.

❋ ❋ ❋

There was a grand welcoming committee for Henry Bardshar on Tuesday, October 15th, 1889. All the old school chums and the neighborhood pals greeted Henry like a long lost brother. Even though he was here for his sister Frona's wedding he squeezed in time to see as many of his friends as he could.

They gathered up in the old barn where they had played Euchre and other card games, what seemed so long ago.

"I haven't been gone a year!" Henry said. "You make it sound as though its been forever."

All the boys grinned. It was great to see Henry again. He had grown taller and heavier not plump, but muscular.

"I'm hard and I'm lean and I'm mean," Henry said, "You fellows grew some yourselves. You shaving yet, Sherwood?"

"Same old Henry," Karl said, "So tell us about the wild west and fighting the Indians."

"Not much to tell," Henry said, "It's rather primitive in Kansas compared to Clyde, but its really wild the farther west you go." He paused. "More trails than roads. Sod huts. I can't wait to go farther west. Eddie's out west. He couldn't make it for Fronie's wedding. He was in Nebraska. Now he's way out in Colorado. That's where I'm heading. Out to be with Ed."

"Wow!" one of the younger boys gasped.

It was less than a year that Mary and Delmar Conger were married and now they were back. And Reverend Conger was to perform the ceremony.

"Next year it's Birdie's turn, " the girls said.

"Not me," Birdie blushed.

The wedding was a pretty home wedding at the Bardshar's on Mechanic Street. It was an evening wedding. Fronie was a lovely bride. About fifty friends and relatives gathered for the ceremony. Rev. S. Delmar Conger officiated and Miss Frons was united in marriage to Mr. W.A. Sheck of Holdredge, Nebraska.

"What is Mr. Sheck's line of work?" one of the guests asked.

"Why don't you know? He's the postmaster at Holdredge."

Henry told Karl and Cliff later as they walked through the streets of the town, "Mary married the preacher. She hung around that young preacher and went to church until she caught him."

He laughed and they kicked through the fallen leaves.

"Then Fronie," Henry continued, with all his exaggerated gestures, "Fronie, pretending to be sooo homesick, and maybe she was, went to the post office every day, looking for a letter from home. And of course, got to know the postmaster."

"Of course," said Cliff.

"Of course," said Karl.

School was out for the summer in early June 1890. Karl didn't attend anymore. Sherwood was in high school. But one day F.M. Ginn, the superintendent invited both Anderson boys to his home to spend the evening.

"Sherwood, soon as you finish your papers, we're supposed to go see Old Man Ginn."

"Fakir Ginn? What for?" Sherwood asked.

Karl shrugged his shoulders. "I got the word at the harness shop. He wants to see both of us as soon as we're free."

The Ginn residence was a large two-story brick on West Buckeye Street. When the boys arrived, Sherwood debated whether to use the front door or go around to the back.

"He said we should come to the side door," Karl said, "He was definite about that."

The two boys climbed the slab stone steps that led to the small porch. It was an open-end side porch with steps leading from both directions. A white-painted spindle railing ran across one side. Ornate gingerbread scrolls decorated the corners of the porch roof. The dark-stained wooden door was massive with a curtained oval window. A doorbell buzzer was built into the door.

Sherwood turned the buzzer. The brothers looked at each other. They had discussed all the possibilities of this visit on the way to the Ginn house. They enumerated mischievous pranks they had performed. They reviewed punishments dealt out by the superintendent. They always came back to the same conclusion: if it were a school punishment, he'd have handled it at school. If it was something that needed parental attention, he'd have had the Major here too.

No, this was something else. "Probably a job needs two people, so he's asking us." Sherwood said.

Francis Marion Ginn came to the door. He was a big, broad-shouldered man, with an enormous black beard. Even though school children referred to him as Old Man Ginn, he was not yet sixty.

"Come in, Boys, come in," Ginn boomed.

Sherwood and Karl entered the doorway, suddenly conscious that they were barefooted. The rich velvety surface of the oriental-type rug felt soft to their feet. Karl and Sherwood glanced around. They had never seen so many books before, all lined up on shelves.

"Sit down, Boys. Sit down," he bellowed again. He motioned to chairs.

The chairs were solid, dark mahogany wood, upholstered in a deep wine color. The boys sunk deep into the centers. Karl felt the velvety surface around the edges of the seat with his fingers.

"You boys are probably wondering why I asked you to come. Probably thought I was going to punish you, eh?"

Karl and Sherwood glanced at each other.

"Not the case," the superintendent answered, "Matter of fact, I keep my switch at the schoolhouse. No, I had other ideas."

He sat back in his favorite armchair, propped his feet up on his footstool and began again.

"This is my library." He stretched out his arms. "My reading room, my sanctuary. You boys like to read, I take it?"

"Yes, Sir," the brothers nodded.

"I've never seen so many books all together before," Sherwood said.

Ginn laughed a hearty, deep belly laugh. "I didn't think you had. This is what I brought you here for. I have all these books. Classics. My two sons have moved on. No one reads these books." He reached out his arms embracing his library. " Charles Dickens, James Fenimore Cooper, Thackeray, Balzac."

"We've got Pilgrim's Progress, Tennyson's Poems and the Bible," Karl said.

"I'm sure you've read those," Ginn said.

"Yes, Sir," the boys answered.

"I want you boys to think about your future. I want you to pursue an education beyond the public schools in Clyde."

"My marks are not good, "Sherwood said.

"We have to be absent a lot," Karl said.

"And tardy," Sherwood added. "See, I've got papers to sell."

"I understand all about that," Ginn said.

Superintendent Ginn shifted himself in his chair and studied the two boys, barefooted, hands clasped in their laps, both well-mannered, both listening intently to the kind patriarch.

He picked up a yellow school pencil and absently turned it end over end, tapping it against his chair arm, smoothing the wood surface of the pencil.

"Karl, you withdrew in March last year," he said, "How old are you?"

"Sixteen, Sir," Karl answered.

"And you, Sherwood?"

"I'll be fourteen in September."

"Yes, it's not too soon to think about your future."

"Extra schooling is expensive. The money we earn helps the family," Karl said.

"Hold on," Ginn said, "If you decide to pursue your studies, the money will be found. I want you to understand this."

Karl and Sherwood remained silent. They didn't understand whether this assistance would be a loan or an outright gift or a scholarship of some sort. They did not ask.

"Now, one of the reasons I asked you to come," Ginn continued, was about this library. Except to clean and dust, no one except myself ever comes into this room, and I get little enough time here. The idea is that you may come and go in this room as you please. Borrow books and return them or read them here. I leave it to you."

Karl and Sherwood looked at each other and then at the kindly schoolmaster.

He continued, "This is to be your library as well as mine. I ask you to come to this side door."

He fished around in his pocket. "Here is the key. It is to be yours. I have a duplicate."

The boys sensed the visit was over and got to their feet. Superintendent Ginn eased himself out of his comfortable chair and stood. He walked the brothers to the door and placed the key in Sherwood's hand.

✼ ✼ ✼

Sherwood was on his way to the racetrack one late summer morning. A wagon drawn by an old black mare clattered to a stop beside Sherwood. It was T.P. Hurd, the grocer, and his wagon.

"Sherwood, my boy," the driver called.

Sherwood waved.

"Climb aboard, my boy," T.P. said, "and ride out into the country with me."

This wasn't the first time such an encounter happened. Sometimes when Sherwood was not busy and there was no school, T.P. Hurd would ask Sherwood if he wanted to ride with him.

Sometimes they'd deliver groceries. T.P. would drive Topsy and the wagon and Sherwood would deliver the orders to the door. Sometimes they just rode out into the country to the Hurd farm south of town.

Sherwood was always eager to go.

"Just you, Sherwood?" Karl asked, "Not Herman, too?"

"Just me," Sherwood said, "Hern doesn't care to go. He gets bored, I guess."

Karl thought a minute. "Probably like us," he said, "Suppose our Pa came along and wanted you to ride with him out in the country. Would you go?"

"Not on your life," Sherwood said, "And hear those same old boring war tales again?"

"Exactly," Karl said. The boys laughed.

T.P. Hurd was a kindly, bearded gentleman. He called Sherwood by his given name, not "Jobby" as his son, Herman did.

"Remind me later." T.P. said, "I've got some things for your mother. It would help me if she could use them. I dislike waste."

"Yes, sir," Sherwood said.

T.P. Hurd sometimes sent over-ripe fruit, slightly damaged produce and day or two-old bakery goods for his mother.

"Such a pleasant day for a drive, Sherwood," T.P. Hurd said.

"Yes, Sir," Sherwood answered.

The road out of town toward the Hurd farm was dusty and full of ruts. Topsy trotted contentedly in the early morning air.

"Do you believe there is a God, my boy?" T.P. Hurd asked Sherwood.

"I hadn't thought about it," Sherwood answered, and he knew what T.P.'s sermon would be on this drive out into the country.

"There is a God, my boy. Don't doubt it," T.P. answered his own question, "but he is not the God of churches."

Sherwood listened, but didn't answer. T.P. gestured with his free hand to the wheat field that had been harvested.

"He is in the field, in that wheat stacked in the field there."

And in a swooping motion of his arm, waved it toward a field of ripe corn.

"He is in every growing stalk of corn."

T.P. pointed to the huge spreading oaks along the roadside.

"He is in the trees."

He patted Sherwood's knee. "He is in you and me."

Sherwood smiled, thinking of what his brother, Karl, had said.

✷ ✷ ✷

One day Toughy McCreery was prowling around Clyde, looking for adventure. And he found it. He looked up his pal, Sherwood to report his discovery.

"Guns! Sherwood."

Together they hiked out to the old McPherson farm. Coffin-like boxes were in the barn. Toughy had pried open one of the boxes and found it contained Civil War rifles. The guns were packed in heavy grease.

"Wow!" Sherwood said.

Toughy told Sherwood he'd been out hunting rabbits. When it began to rain, he ducked into the old McPherson barn for shelter. That barn area had been neglected and bushes and brambles grew up around it. He spotted the boxes.

Toughy said to Sherwood, "What if you could take this gun, saw it off and use it for hunting?"

"Yeah, What if?" Sherwood said.

"Well, Sherwood," Toughy said, "I went to see Carter. You know Carter?"

Sherwood said he did. Carter had a shop and he repaired lawn mowers.

Toughy continued. "Carter said that he could transform a rifle such as this into a shot gun at a cost of twenty-five cents."

"Wow!" Sherwood said.

"And then he asked me where I got this rifle."

"You tell him, Toughy?"

"'Course not."

Sherwood and Toughy bantered back and forth.

Where did these guns come from?

Who do they belong to?

Sherwood had so many questions and no answers. He thought possibly they belonged to the government.

"Would it be stealing to take these guns?"

"Well, they'll only rust here in the barn," Toughy said.

"Not the way they are packed in that heavy grease," said Sherwood.

After a quiet spell, Toughie said, "Instead of going to all the trouble of getting the barrel sawed off to make a shot gun, lets just sell the whole gun for fifty cents! We could split the profits."

So the boys sold a few rifles. There were mishaps. Accidents. Emma Anderson learned of the adventure and squelched it.

Sometime later, the boys learned that the Civil War rifles were to be used as a picket fence around the statue of General McPherson in the cemetery. The fence was never constructed. No one knew what became of the rifles.

✳ ✳ ✳

Sherwood had driven Old Topsy, T.P. Hurd's horse and wagon around the country to deliver groceries. And for that, he collected pocket change.

He had saved his delivery money along with money from other odd jobs and his newspaper savings. One day he made an important purchase. He bought a bicycle. It was a second-hand bicycle, but a bicycle none the less.

'A bicycle!" Karl exclaimed.

"It's an investment." Sherwood answered. "I need it

for my paper business. I can cut my time delivering in half. This bicycle will pay for itself." He went on, "Also, I can run errands and make small, quick drop-offs at people's houses or other stores for T.P. Hurd. And some of the others in town."

Bicycles were not that common, but were becoming more and more popular. Now, Sherwood had his own. He fitted it up with a basket for carrying newspapers, small boxes and bundles. He was quite successful the summer of 1891.

Sherwood usually had a few coins in his pocket to jingle. Herman Hurd never had any spending money and he said so. So Sherwood treated his friend, Hern to a dish of ice cream, but he asked for two spoons so they could share the dish.

Ice cream was a new dessert at the time and Mrs. H. Baker served it at her restaurant. Mrs. H. Baker, or Rowena had several sons and daughters who helped her at the bakery and restaurant. Her daughter, Jennie was a classmate of both boys. She'd come over to the table where they were and would talk a minute. She was pretty and lively and they didn't mind the visit. One day, Jennie coyly asked Sherwood about his bicycle.

"Jobby, she said, I've decided to learn to ride." She giggled. Sherwood and Herman looked up. She went on.

"But unfortunately, I have no bicycle."

She giggled again and they waited.

"Sooo, I was wondering," she said. "If I could possibly borrow yours?"

"Sure," Sherwood didn't hesitate. "It's parked outside."

She pulled up a chair and sat next to them at the little ice cream table.

"Well, not just this minute. I don't want anybody watching."

"Okay," Sherwood said.

He didn't have a problem with this. He was always willing to help. So Sherwood left his bicycle with Jennie and he and Herman walked on home.

"Where's your wheel?" Karl asked.

"I lent it to Jennie Baker," Sherwood said.

"Why?" Karl asked. And Sherwood told him about the conversation.

"I hope you get it back," Karl said, "And in one piece."

"Don't worry," Sherwood said, "I'll get it tomorrow, or the next day."

But he did worry. A week went by, and then another. Sherwood needed his bicycle. He'd become used to it and he depended on it.

"Some nerve," he stewed. "She doesn't deliver newspapers. She doesn't deliver parcels."

Sherwood had reached the limit of his schoolboy generosity. And early one morning, before Jennie was up, on his way to the depot, he went around to the rear of the Baker place and confiscated his own bicycle

❋ ❋ ❋

Sherwood sat in his civics class and stared out the window. Recitations were going on and Sherwood heard them, but he was off in his own world.

The room was filled with the same group of boys he had gone to school with for years: Will Bacon, Moody Dwight, Clark Wilder, Mack Robinson, John Botsford, and Herman Hurd. Sherwood's seat was near the rear of the room. He could lean forward and look across and see Herman Hurd. They had a system of hand signals to pass messages to each other.

There were girls in the room who had gone all through school with Sherwood: Florence Mugg, Mabel Supner and the two Jennie B's; Jennie Baker and Jennie Bemis.

He could see Jennie Bemis across the room, near Herman Hurd. She was drumming her fingers quietly on her desk, mentally practicing her piano lesson, silently tapping her toes.

He could see Jennie Baker in one of the front seats, sitting up straight with her hands folded on her desk. She was as attentive as ever. Her hair was braided and a wide ribbon bow was fastened across the back of her head. Her dress with its sailor collar was pressed and starched.

Sherwood gazed around the room. The old clock ticked on the wall. George Washington looked down from his picture above the blackboard. The heavy green shades on the windows were raised to let in the early winter sun.

Sherwood looked at the bare branches of the Maple trees and wished for spring. He barely noticed the teacher walk to the back of the room. The teacher stopped at a desk several seats in front of him to reprimand a girl.

When the teacher's voice became loud, Sherwood took notice. He could see him shake his finger at the girl and he wondered what she had done to deserve this castigation. Evidently she answered him in a way he didn't like. The teacher slapped the girl.

Sherwood jumped up. His book fell to the floor. His face was flushed. He was furious.

"Don't you hit her again!" he shouted.

The teacher stepped back.

Later, after school, Jennie Baker asked him about the incident.

"Sherwood, what happened?"

Sherwood shrugged it off, but he had been disturbed about the incident.

❋ ❋ ❋

Karl was finished with school in Clyde. It was time to move on. He took the train to Cleveland to work during the day and go to art school at night.

Busy Times in Town

The McPherson Guard made the arrangements for a production, which was held the last of February 1892 at the Opera House. It was billed as a military comedy-drama.

The Tichenors were both involved in the entertainment as they were in most of the musical programs in the area. J.B. and Maggie had the leading roles. J.B.'s brother, George played the part of General Sherman.

Sherwood had the role of "Little Jimmy" in the five-part play.

"Allatoona" was a selection from French's Standard Drama Series. One citizen who had the play-book remarked, "I don't see where there is a character in here by the name of Little Jimmy. Who is Little Jimmy?"

Another explained as best he could that J.B. or one of the others wrote in the extra part for Sherwood. Sherwood was fifteen and he added the youthful touch needed for the show.

❋ ❋ ❋

Auntie Lucy Fisher lived at 133 Arch Street. She catered for 24 of the younger set at her home. She treated them to a grand supper such as only she could provide and the guests presented her with a fine chair.

"It was some party," Herman Hurd said to Sherwood later, "The whole gang was there, Clarence Whittaker, Jimmie Moore, Will Bacon, Dean Richmond..."

"Any girls?"

"Oh, sure," Herman answered, "the Jennie B's, Mabel Supner, Pearl Mann, Caddie McCleary, all of them. Too bad you couldn't go."

"I was invited," Sherwood said, "but I promised J. B. I'd be in the play. So I was kind of busy last Friday evening."

✸ ✸ ✸

On a March Friday preceding spring vacation, the pupils of the high school gave a concert program at Terry's Hall. This entertainment was for the purpose of raising funds to purchase books for the school library. There were recitations and songs.

Sherwood took part in the evening program. His recitation was titled, "The Schoolmaster's Guest." He spoke to a crowded house. There was standing room only.

One of Sherwood's schoolmates, Clark Wilder, in a clear tenor voice, sang, "Sweet Genevieve," and Chella Hutchinson recited, "Trouble in the Amen Corner." There was a chorus of sixty voices.

"All this talent in our little town."

"We can be mighty proud of our school children," were comments that were heard.

✸ ✸ ✸

The boys were old enough to organize their own entertainment as well. On June 27, 1892, a Monday, Scott Crockett was eighteen years old and he gave himself a birthday party at his parents' country home on

Butternut Ridge. Forty or more of his young friends assembled to celebrate the occasion.

The good-natured Rat Gould and his assistant were on hand with fiddle and dulcimer and the evening was given up to dancing and free and unrestrained social enjoyment.

Shortly after midnight an elegant supper was served.

❋ ❋ ❋

By early September 1892, the Wilder Brothers & Estill had finished their sauerkraut plant. It was built just west of the piano factory between the Lake Shore and W. & L.E. railroads. Ten workmen had been at work on the plant to get it ready for operation. Machinery had been moved in.

Now in September, the owners planned to run the factory night and day with a dozen men to take care of the cabbage. By the end of September, the Wilder Brothers & Estill's sauerkraut factory was running full blast. Their acreage was contracted for 100 acres and they were producing over 130 barrels of kraut a day.

The factory wasn't able to keep up with the cabbage being harvested. Wagonloads of cabbage piled high pulled up to the factory to be unloaded. A request for boys to help went out.

"Lets give her a try," Irve said, "It can't be any worse than planting the dang cabbages."

So Irve and Sherwood trudged down to Wilder Brothers & Estill's. There were sixteen men and boys employed and the kraut factory ran on double time, or until 10 p.m. every day and turned out 200 barrels of kraut per day.

One evening Sherwood and Irve, their clothes reeking, soaking wet, chilled to the bone, shed part of their clothes and boots on the back porch.

"We plant the cabbages. We harvest the cabbages and we stomp them to death." Irve said.

"Sauerkraut stomping. There's got to be an easier way," Sherwood said.

It looked as though there would be a long and prosperous reign for the company. One of the cabbage farmers for the Wilder & Estill plant was Jacob LeFever. He had acres of cabbage. He sold a load in which there were 308 heads. The load weighed more than a ton. Some of the heads weighed over twenty pounds apiece.

Probably, the biggest load of cabbage belonged to George Welliver. It weighed 6280 lbs. The price of cabbage was high.

"I think its good times for us all." One of the cabbage men commented.

"And a good time for a kraut factory in Clyde," another said.

Wilder & Estill had a cold storage warehouse as well as a retail store. Willie helped them invoice their goods the first of the year.

Willie Wilder left for Portland, Oregon on January 11th. He had expected to remain in Clyde a few days longer, but started out Wednesday night in the midst of bad weather. His brother-in-law, K.S. Breckenridge wired him that he was needed.

"The old place has changed since I left Clyde," Willie had told Karl before Karl took the train to Cleveland. "Dad's really into sauerkraut."

Karl laughed. "So was Sherwood and Irve," he said.

❊ ❊ ❊

Ex-president Rutherford B. Hayes, who had retired to his home in Fremont, died on Tuesday, January 17th. Schools were closed on Friday. Teachers and many pupils attended the funeral. President Grover Cleveland traveled 2000 miles in the inclement weather to attend. His train passed through Clyde to and from Fremont and Clyde folks gathered at the station to catch a glimpse of the President.

❊ ❊ ❊

Sherwood worked in the back room at the *Enterprise*. There was always someone coming in with news of the day and Sherwood lived for excitement. Sherwood also worked at the horse stables throughout the year, although he was busier in summer and during the racing season than in the winter. Horses were fed, groomed, exercised and he tended to these duties along with several other swipes.

Sherwood didn't have a steady girlfriend, but he often squired Mabel Supner. Mabel's father, George was a cabinetmaker and the family of girls lived on Duane Street. Sherwood and Mabel went to dancing school together and on sleigh rides in the company of other friends, Herman Hurd, Johnny Botsford, the two Jennie B's The winter was ideal for sleighing.

In late January, Sherwood, Herman Hurd and others in a sleighing party headed for a dance in Bellevue. It was a Saturday, early in the afternoon. They were dressed in their Sunday best and started off in high spirits.

While they were tripping the light fantastic, the weather turned warmer. The sun came out. The thermometer reached a record 38 degrees. The snow melted. The sleigh was of no use. Part of the company had to remain in Bellevue, while one of the young men rode off to fetch help.

T.P. Hurd came with a wagon. Herman and the others clambered aboard and rode to Clyde.

Somehow Sherwood missed the ride and was stranded in Bellevue. He had to walk the entire distance of eight miles through the slush to Clyde. His dancing slippers were ruined. He was furious. When he arrived in town he scolded his friend roundly.

"You'll get over it, Jobby," Herman said, "You always do."

※ ※ ※

There was a gathering place for young people in Green Springs. Some called it a Dancing Parlor and some called it a Resort. It was referred to as Ford and Rainy's. Green Spring was five miles west of Clyde. In the spring or summer or fall, it was a pleasant drive. In the winter with ice and snow, it could be treacherous. If there was a party at Ford and Rainy's, inclement weather didn't deter young people from making the trip.

Sherwood attended the dances frequently with his friends, Herman, Johnny Botsford, and others. He sometimes escorted Mabel Supner. He wrote her brief notes addressing them, "Friend Mabel" and invited her to accompany him.

Occasionally, Herman drove the sleigh and Sherwood, John Botsford, Clarence Whittaker, and other friends rode with him. Sometimes the girls went with them, Mabel Supner, Lucy Hurd and the two Jennie B.'s.

On one occasion, Mabel wasn't able to go with them. Sherwood wrote Mabel later.

"I wish you girls could have gone up to the dance. We had a regular circus. Herman could not dance. He hurt his foot coming over so he went home early. John and I did not get home until about two o'clock."

❋ ❋ ❋

Sherwood was familiar with horses. He knew horses as well as any boy his age. He knew their dispositions, their special likes and dislikes, but he was not a horseman.

Herman had a horse and a new sleigh and he had taken his girl for a ride. He asked Sherwood if he wanted to take his girl for a ride. The streets were snowy, but not dangerous.

Sherwood took the reins. They trotted down Cherry Street. The horse was eager to get home, and recognizing his home territory, began to run and upset both Sherwood and his girl on the Cherry Street corner.

His girl laughed. No one was hurt but Sherwood was embarrassed.

❋ ❋ ❋

Cliff Paden's cousin, Bob Jones, had become good friends with Karl and had been encouraging him to look into attending the Art School in Chicago. On one of

Karl's visits to Clyde, the two friends bumped into each other.

This time Karl had an agenda. He had planned to enroll in the spring term. He had scrutinized the catalogues and literature Bob passed on to him and with careful calculations, Karl figured he could attend the evening classes easily and also take the day classes probably two months out of the year. The spring term started the middle of March.

"Look up my cousin, Frank Lay," Bob Jones said, "I'm sure you'd be welcome to stay with him." He gave Karl the address.

"And one more thing," Bob reached into his pocket for his wallet and pulled out three five-dollar bills and handed them to Karl.

"What's this for?" Karl was bewildered.

"It's an investment, Karl," Bob said, "Fifteen dollars in advance. I want an early oil painting. Just a small one, after you get settled in Chicago."

"Are you serious?" Karl looked at the bills in disbelief.

"Completely serious. Put them in your pocket. And remember the investment."

Karl smiled. "I won't forget," he said.

❈ ❈ ❈

Cliff had nearly as many jobs as Sherwood. He helped at the *Enterprise*. He taught school and he also had his church duties and responsibilities. He had taught the winter term in the Lay school district, south of Clyde. Through his persuasion the directors of the district erected a flagstaff and purchased a fine eight-foot bunting flag, which was flung to the breeze for the first time on Washington's Birthday.

Then in the middle of March, he abruptly resigned his teaching position and accepted a job with a printing office in Tiffin. Cliff's cousin, Scott Crockett, who had been teaching at District No. 4 in Adams Township, finished his winter term and was engaged for the spring term to finish out Cliff's school year in the Lay District.

Cliff was quite busy with his church responsibilities. He was the Lay Reader for the Grace Episcopal Church in Clyde and he was involved with the upcoming Easter service

On March 12th 1893, Cliff and the minister of St. Paul's in Fremont exchanged churches. Cliff delivered a strong sermon and engaged the attention of the whole congregation.

"His reading was good. His emphasis was right and his manner was dignified and reverential," one of the elder parishioners said.

"We wish him a bright future," another said.

❉ ❉ ❉

The waterworks trustees prepared to make improvements at the pumping station. Besides extending the system, they proposed drilling new wells. They planned to make the supply of artesian water so plentiful that there would be no danger of scarcity of water during the summer droughts.

With good weather the Buckeye sewer project was finally underway. Tom Forgerson hoped to complete the project as rapidly as possible.

Sherwood and Irve were water boys.

"It will give us a few coins to jingle, Sherwood," Irve said, "And it can't be as bad as the strawberries or the sauerkraut stomping."

Shortly after Grover Cleveland entered the White House in 1893, the country faced a major depression. On May 5th, the stocks fell sharply on the New York Stock Exchange. A world wide financial panic began. Railroads began to go into bankruptcy. The steel industry declined and the banking system was strained. People were out of work and job-seekers flocked to Chicago, hoping there would be employment at the Columbian Exposition.

Cliff left Clyde for Chicago on Sunday, May 14th just before a hard thunderstorm. His sister Carrie left Tiffin for Chicago a week later. By the end of May, all the Padens had settled there. And Karl Anderson was there, too.

Back in Clyde, the thunderstorm Cliff missed was destructive. Jennie Baker told Sherwood, Herman Hurd and Jennie Bemis about it. They were walking together on Main Street.

Lightning struck the Baker residence on Main and Cherry. It made a hole under the eave-trough went into the kitchen, set fire to papers and a broom, knocked holes in the tin-ware. The Baker family put the flames out before much damage was done.

"I never was so frightened before in my life," Jennie said, "And it's a wonder the house didn't burn to the ground and burn us all!"

Jennie Bemis sympathized with Jennie Baker. She had been through a fire scare earlier. They talked for a few minutes and one of them asked Herman about his brother's wedding.

Charles Hurd married his long time girl friend, Miss Agnes Barton at the home of her grandmother in Green Spring. The Green Spring Band serenaded the couple.

"Mush." Herman Hurd said to Sherwood and the girls, "They're going to live on Cherry Street in Terry's double house."

"S.M. Terry got bit," Sherwood said.

Herman Hurd looked up. "By what?"

"Free Tuttle's dog bit him and he's looking for the brute with a gun," Sherwood said, "Or so I heard."

❋ ❋ ❋

Sherwood had his job at Tom Whiteheads and Frank Harvey's stables, and his friend Johnny Botsford worked at Nichols & Bemis' Livery barn. The boys, along with Herman Hurd, all school friends went over to Bellevue. They had a grand time at the fair, and remained until late at night. They intended to come home on the Lake Shore train No 9.

The train whistle blew and the boys raced to catch it. Johnny Botsford tripped on a switch and fell. He got up, jumped on the train and came home.

"You okay, Johnny?" the boys in turn asked.

"Yeah, sure," Johnny said, "Skinned my knee. Hurt my shoulder."

"You don't look so good," one said.

On arriving in Clyde, his companions took him to Doctor E.W. Baker's. He had a broken collarbone.

"I didn't realize I was hurt that bad," Johnny said.

The boys took him to his parents, who lived in Mrs. M.W. Taylor's house on Maple Street.

"It was a narrow escape for the lad and should be a warning to youngsters to be careful when around the cars," Ben Jackson, the editor said.

❋ ❋ ❋

"There were so many shady deals going on in Clyde the first part of March, 1894, it was hard to find the sun," one of the old-timers said.

There was the gray-whiskered picture-enlarging scheme. A supposed representative of a Chicago Art firm took cash for orders for pictures to be enlarged and was never seen again.

There was the Kandy Kitchen downfall, where one of the partners absconded with a forged check.

And there was the Soap Scam.

It happened on the streets of Clyde, March 3rd. It was Saturday and the streets were blocked with people. A loud-mouthed individual with a broken-down banjo attracted a big crowd at the post office corner.

After the usual preliminaries this brash individual introduced his specialty.

"Folks, step up! See the wonder of this new, never-before-seen soap, a miraculous soap. It's guaranteed to wash printers' towels clean. No more ink stains."

The crowd stared at him in open delight. They roared at his crude jests and alleged humor and crowded closer. They relished the suspense and the hawker waited until the crowd was in the mood to buy.

"Only fifteen cents for the Miracle Soap," he said, "A mere fifteen cents."

"I want one," cried one.

"Give me two pieces," said another.

The loudmouthed person with the broken-down banjo collected the money, doled out the little cakes of white soap as fast as he conveniently could until his stock was depleted. The people were happy, almost ecstatic with their purchases.

Later, Sherwood and Herman told the story of the Miraculous Soap to T.P. Hurd. T.P. Hurd laughed.

"The poor suckers," he said, "Boys, people are gullible. People are trusting. They want to believe what the man is telling them. They are carried away on their emotions."

The boys stared at T.P. Hurd, his great bushy beard, a kindly man, warning them of the unscrupulousness of some so-called salesmen.

"I sold the soap to the fellow, myself. Six cakes for a quarter. It's plain, ordinary house soap. The sharper simply cut the cakes in two, wrapped a clean paper about them and sold them to the suckers for fifteen cents a cake."

"Thirty cents a cake," the boys were quick with their arithmetic. "A dollar-eighty for six cakes for which he had only paid a quarter. One dollar fifty-five cents clean profit."

"Don't get any ideas, Boys," T.P. Hurd said. "Sharpers like that one always pay for their shady dealings sooner or later."

After the crowd on Saturday, and the Sunday churchgoers, horses and buggies and wagons clattered up and down the streets.

By Monday morning, the streets presented the appearance of a country barnyard. And the hoe and broom brigade went to work and cleaned it up. Now, Main Street was respectable once more.

✸ ✸ ✸

With Coxey's Army on the March and talk of unemployment, Clyde, itself seemed unaffected by the labor troubles. In fact much of Clyde focused on baseball.

A large number of spectators flocked to Ames Field on Friday afternoon, May 4th 1894 to watch the game between the High School Nine and the Town Nine. The school board had prohibited athletic teams so a group of the high school boys formed their own team to play after school and on Saturdays.

A diamond had been laid out on the sod at Ames Field. Even though recent rains made the conditions of the ground very bad, a good game was played.

Herman Hurd, Turkey Clapp with Curtis Harter pitching and Norris Sowell catching made up part of the team. Sherwood did not play.

The Town Nine won the game 15 to 31.

"We got some pretty good ball players in Clyde. We could organize a club and play other towns," one of the ball players said, "Maybe call it the Clyde Stars."

Sherwood, of course was one of the organizers.

"Jobby, you can't play," Herman Hurd announced at an organized meeting, "You can't catch a ball to save your life."

"I like baseball," Sherwood said.

"If you play, we'll lose every game," Herman, who was a proven first baseman added.

"Let Jobby be manager," one of the others said, "He can go along with us."

It was a unanimous decision. Sherwood and Clarence Whittaker, who couldn't play ball either, were named managers.

Most of the young men were in high school. Some had dropped out to find jobs. All were in their late teens. A few of the players preferred certain positions: Herman Hurd, first base; Clark Wilder, second; Barley Mann at third base, shortstop, Ralph Hiner with Willie Sargeant, Waxey Sellinger and Toughie McCreery fielders.

There was a wide range of pitchers coming and going. Substitutions were made at the last minute due to work schedules or other problems.

The team members wore uniforms consisting of dark knickers, light colored sweaters with a star within a circle, and of course, baseball caps. The managers wore shirts, ties, vests, jackets and bowler hats.

There was the news that Bellevue had organized a baseball club and wanted to play the Clyde nine.

"The question is," one of the Clyde players said, "Will the Bellevue boys keep sober if they come over here?"

Baseball was all the rage nowadays. There was a game between Clyde and Bellevue scheduled for three in the afternoon of Thursday, May 17th.

"The admission is free and everyone is invited and we'll have a grand time unless the Bellevue team flunks again," one of the Clyde players said.

People who had been complaining that Spring about a lack of rain, needn't complain any longer. Rain fell almost constantly from Thursday, May 17th to Tuesday May 22nd and the ground was thoroughly soaked. Games were postponed. They were rescheduled.

On May 24th, the Clyde Stars went over to Bellevue and played a game on the fairgrounds with the Bellevue Club. They played hard and long and when the last out was made and the game was officially over, that warm May day, the Clyde Stars waved farewell to the Bellevue team as they boarded their wagon for home, Bellevue players called back, "Wait 'til next time!"

The Clyde ballplayers were in a jubilant mood. For six innings the Bellevue players couldn't score a run and the Clyde Stars won the game by a score of 14 to 9.

Brownie Ellis, the batboy picked up the Stars' bats and slid them into a gunny sack and tossed them into the wagon.

"That was a pretty good drubbing we gave Bellevue!" second baseman Clark Wilder grinned.

"Sure was," Norris Sowell agreed, swinging his catchers mask.

"That was some game," the Stars said to each other.

"And I feel pretty good about the $1.50 ball we brought home with us," one of the players said.

"That too," the others answered.

The boys chattered to each other as the wagon jounced along the Pike toward Clyde.

"Yeah, I sure do enjoy whippin' those guys from Bellevue," Toughie McCreery gloated, "Whoopee!" He tossed his cap in the air and caught it. "Whoopee!"

The others agreed. Talk shifted to the next game coming up. Was it a Fremont game? Or would it be with Tiffin?

"Which is it, Jobby? You got the schedule."

"Don't have it with me. I'll let you know," Sherwood said.

"Some manager you are," Waxy Sellinger, who played center kidded.

"Ah, Jobby's got things on his mind," his best friend Herman explained.

Sherwood waved his hand to dismiss the talk.

"Come on home with me to supper, Jobby."

"I don't know, Hern."

"Ma's made pies."

"Count me in."

"Me too. Me too." The others echoed and laughed as they broke up on Main Street.

Sherwood and Herman Hurd cut diagonally across Main Street toward West Cherry. At the Hurd house, Sherwood stopped.

"Hern, I'm going on home. Thanks for the invitation to supper. Some other time."

"Sure, Jobby," Herman said.

Sherwood rarely refused supper at his place.

"I just feel I better get home. Stella depends on me."

"I understand," Herman said and waved a good-bye, Sherwood went on down the street.

❋ ❋ ❋

On July 4th, 1899 at one o'clock in the morning, nightwatch Elijah Scott discovered a fire in the Dewey Block, occupied by Jackson & Sons hardware store. Immediately he turned in the alarm. The fire laddies had scarcely got their hose in shape and had begun to throw water into the building when an open can of powder in the cellar exploded. It blew a hole in the floor and shattered the entire glass front of the store and nearly injured several firemen.

There was considerable combustible material in the cellar, including gunpowder, gasoline, oils and paint materials. The work of the firemen was very hazardous.

The flames seemed to be in a dozen places at once and the entire building was on fire. Fortunately the cellar soon became so flooded that there was no further damage from explosions, but the most strenuous efforts were required to keep the fire under control and prevent its spreading. Four streams of water were kept constantly playing on the fire until it was finally subdued. The firemen battled the fire until seven a.m.

The origin of the fire was unknown. All of the occupants of the Dewey Block were obliged to find other quarters. The building was totally unfit for occupancy.

After the disastrous fire, W.H. Jackson sent the entire fire department, the Hose Company and the Hook and Ladder Company to the Nichols House for breakfast.

"I never heard the alarm," Alf Granger said, "I hope you'll excuse me for not being on hand to help out the fire."

He was making ice cream every day at the Granger Bros.

"I could have taken a dish of my splendid ice cream to the fire," he said. "The effect would have been chilling enough to avert the catastrophe."

The boys of the town were out in full force to inspect the damage of the Dewey Block. They lamented that it occurred during the night while they were asleep and they missed all the excitement.

❉ ❉ ❉

Sherwood was working at Richards & Co,. the dry goods store. He also delivered for T.P. Hurd, and he worked at the livery stables. Sometimes he accompanied the horse owners to races.

"Tom Whitehead's trotter, "Solarion" was the horse to watch." Sherwood announced. He raced in Tiffin, but there were sixteen horses on the track and Solarion drew twelfth place to start. He didn't do well.

Sherwood went with the Clyde Stars every chance he got. They went to Oak Harbor to play the Swamp Angels on Sunday, July 1st. The Stars lost by a score of 16 to 23.

"Rank umpiring's what made us lose," Toughy McCreery said.

"I can think of a few people who'd say we lost because we played baseball on Sunday," another of the players said.

On the Fourth of July, Bellevue's team known as the Nine Spots came over to play the Clyde Stars.

"Those Bellevue players think they can beat the stuffing out of us," One of the Clyde Stars said.

The Fourth of July crowd at Clyde was large and exuberant. They cheered and whooped it up. The game was played for six innings and Clyde won 12 to 28. The Bellevue team was terribly broken up.

"I thought they were gonna cry," one of the Clyde players said.

"Yeah," said another, "And then they holler, 'Wait 'till next time.'"

And the next time it was Clyde's turn to go to Bellevue. The Clyde Stars were trounced 23 to 14.

✳ ✳ ✳

On July 21st, 1894 a Saturday evening about dusk, a dusty traveler astride an old gray nag rode into Clyde. He asked to see the mayor.

"I am Count Joseph Bylakowski in command of the 'steenth Division of the U.S. Industrial Army," he said to Mayor Sprague.

"Where are you going? Where is your army going? Who commissioned you?" were some of the questions the mayor asked.

"My army of 152 men is camped in Arthur Clapp's grove west of town. We'll reach Clyde about 8 o'clock tomorrow morning," he said. "We expect the village to furnish breakfast. A loaf of bread, half a pound of meat, a pint of coffee with a little sugar for each man."

The mayor was bewildered. At once he summoned the council.

Most of the councilmen had heard of this so-called army before.

"Are they dangerous? Just what did they do?" asked one.

"Thievery. Mischief. At Fremont they took possession of the fairgrounds without permission, camping there overnight, breaking into halls and befouling them, using the fairground fence for fuel, stealing chickens and clothing from adjoining residences," said one of the councilmen. "They were driven out of town."

Clyde Mayor Sprague called on Co.I, 16th ONG to stand by to meet any emergency that might arise. The fire bell rang 4 – 4 – 4, which was the military riot call for the militia to quell a disturbance.

At eight o'clock on Sunday morning, the Count's army marched into town on Maumee Pike. Marshal Alexander Harnden and special policeman S.D. West met the army at Main Street. As they turned up Main Street the marshal undertook to stop them, telling them they could not come into town, but must pass on through. They paid little attention to him, but marched right along.

"We will march into town and we will have bread or blood," said the Count.

"You will get no bread from the town but will find lots of blood if you persist," the marshal told him and he waved his hand as a signal.

Captain William E. Gillett with 25 men of Co. I, who had been near at hand in case of emergency, formed across Main Street a few rods ahead of the invading army, with guns loaded and bayonets fixed.

The Count's army stopped short, and a few of the men skedaddled, but most of them masses at once around their leader, as though they had been well-trained in that movement. Half a dozen of them made a break for adjoining houses, but the marshal, Winchester in hand, followed them and chased them out of town.

After a few moments parleying, the Count, seeing he would not be permitted to come into town, agreed to march his men to the eastern outskirts of the village.

"Now, after you have your army outside the corporation limit, you and your wife may come back into the village and get what money and provision sympathizing friends may wish to donate," the marshal told the Count.

Co.I formed in the rear of the army and escorted them to the corporation line and remained on duty there until the army started for Bellevue. Several hundred citizens were also on hand to see the fun and render assistance if necessary.

The boys of the town whooped and hollered and joined in the excitement.

The mayor was criticized. Thoughtless persons said that he had no right to call out State Troops, that it would have been cheaper to feed the army.

"Mayor Sprague had a perfect right under the statutes to call out the soldiers," said one of the councilmen. "The pay for the soldiers comes from the State, not the village."

The Count's army was composed mostly of Poles and Prussians.

The Count's wife made a speech to the crowd.

"We are anarchists," she said in broken English, and she asserted that the whole army were selling an anarchist book in which was given instructions for making dynamite, Greek Fire, and bombs.

"They left a book at the *Enterprise*," Ben Jackson said, "It's the worst kind of anarchist doctrine from beginning to end."

More and more stories about Count Bylakowski's Army were told and repeated. Clyde had not had such a topic of conversation for a long time, not since the Fourth of July fire in the Dewey Block.

"Did you notice their clubs?" one citizen said, "Nearly every man in the army carried a heavy club, many were tipped with iron. What were they for?"

"What about the dog?" another said.

"A member of that Polish Army had a fine dog he was leading by a rope. I believe it was Harry Tuck, one of the reporters, anyway, who asked him about the dog. The fellow says, 'Oh, he's been with us ever since Chicago'."

His companion laughed. "Probably stolen."

"Yes. Turns out that the fellow stole the dog in Fremont and the owner reclaimed it in Cleveland. He had the thief jailed."

"Good," the townsman said. "Every place they have stopped, they've shown their fiendishness. They should be sentenced to bread and water for six months."

✻ ✻ ✻

In early August, Karl was home from Chicago on a visit. Sherwood gave Karl the grand tour and in his way, told all the bits and pieces of the lives of those involved.

"Now, you come to Chicago, Sherwood, and I'll show you around." Karl said.

❋ ❋ ❋

Stella planned a lawn party for her brother. She was an expert at arranging parties. She had helped with church socials and with schoolgirl teas and going-away parties. Stella's budget for decorating and purchasing refreshments was small, but she was creative. She used common grasses and wildflowers and ferns from the backyard by Sucker Run for her floral decorations.

Her food selection was also simple, but tasteful. Jennie Baker's mother offered her services, but with around thirty guests, Stella felt she could handle everything.

Stella had invited those of Karl's friends she knew to be in town. Willie Wilder was back from Portland, Oregon. Bob Jones, Scott Crockett, Wynne Ames, Moody Dwight, all in town. Sherwood's friends: Herman Hurd, of course, Barley Mann, John Botsford.

Many of Stella's girl friends and girls her brothers knew also were on the guest list.

The evening was warm. Stella, with Irve and Ray's help had hung Japanese lanterns in the trees and they swayed slightly in the breeze. She had a refreshment table with lemonade on a long table she'd borrowed from the church. Also extra chairs. There was fiddle music.

Emma sat on the porch and watched the festivities. Friends and neighbors visited with her as they sipped lemonade

"So how was Portland ?" Karl asked Willie Wilder and the two talked about their homes away from home, their work and families.

Willie's sister, Helen, now Mrs. Breckenridge, and her husband had moved back from Oregon to Toledo.

"Dad and Mom, of course got on the train immediately and went to Toledo for a visit," Willie said.

"Of course," Karl laughed.

There were snippets of conversation all around. Johnny Botsford was helping out at *The Reporter* office. Bob Jones, who was in town, came to the gathering. So did his cousins, Bessie Lay and the Crocketts.

"It could be a cousin party, too," one of the group said. "About all we need is Cliff." Cliff was in Chicago.

At times like this, Karl missed Henry Bardshar. His brother, Willie, who was at the party gave a report on Henry, who was doing well in the West.

The Supner girls, Mabel, and Maude came. Harriet Day, who'd been visiting her sister Ida, Mrs. William Gillett, the two Jennie B's, the Wyatt girls, Hallie McCleary, the Buzzell girls, all anxious to see Karl.

The first part of the week Karl was uptown. He poked his head in at Miller's Tailor Shop. Johnny Becker was arranging packets of shirts on the shelves.

"Some party, Karl," Johnny said, "It was great to see everyone."

Karl smiled. Johnny went on. "Willie Wilder has grown older."

"We all have," Karl answered and looked around. "You making changes here?"

"Guess you haven't heard," Johnny Becker said, "We were robbed." He went on to tell Karl what happened. "Miller thought I forgot to lock the door. Elijah Scott, the nightwatch found the back door open and notified Miller, who gave him the key and asked him to lock the door."

Karl looked up, interested.

"So I come in next morning, not knowing about the door and key and all. What do I find? Some burgler carried away three pairs of pants, three vests and three overcoats."

"Sounds as though there were three burglers and they needed new outfits," Karl said.

"Other goods, which were hung in plain sight were not disturbed," Johnny said, pointing to the racks of clothes. "Marshal Harnden thinks that local talent is responsible."

"Zan Harnden will catch them." Karl was ready to go.

"Tell your brother I got some new reading material in," Johnny Becker said.

Karl nodded. "I'll do that."

❋ ❋ ❋

Friday, August 10th was a special evening in Clyde. Scott Crockett, who attended Tri-State Normal College in Angola, Indiana, was a member of the male Star Quartet. He brought the Star Quartet to the K. of P. Hall for a concert.

It was an evening to remember. The hall was filled. Besides the offering by the quartet, there were soloists. Misses Stella Niles, Bessie Lay, Fred Clark, and Frank

Crockett, Jr. There were Piano Solos of Misses Laura Saulsbury and Jennie Bemis.

Frank Crockett, Sr. and his two sons, Frank, Jr. and Scott, whose rendition of "The Bonny Green Fields of Corn brought down the house and it was loudly re-demanded.

While Karl was in Clyde, he tried to see everything that was going on in town. When they were both in Chicago, Bessie Lay joked with Karl.

"You'll probably have to go to Clyde to hear me sing," she said. And it was true.

✳ ✳ ✳

By October most of the tomato crop was harvested. The canning companies were running full tilt. Tomatoes were still being canned. The Clyde Canning Company put out a request for 20,000 bushels of good paring apples. Apple canning gave employment to about a hundred residents of Clyde. Kraut was being processed and the bicycle factory was gearing up for a November start-up.

The baseball season was over.

"Probably a good thing it is over for the Clyde Stars, anyway," Herman Hurd said. "Waxy Sellinger moved away and Toughy McCreery broke his leg."

Frank McCreery, or Toughy, as he was called, jumped from a train in Green Spring and broke his leg. He was brought to Clyde to be attended to and taken to Elijah Scott's home. The Women's Relief Corps was looking after his comfort.

"It's the least we can do," one of the ladies said, "His father was an old soldier."

Most of the boys had left school without graduating. Herman was the only boy to graduate in his class. He didn't need to earn a living and his father wouldn't have permitted it anyway. Sherwood's mother had died and now that Karl was away, Jobby needed to earn more than spondulkies. He needed real money. He left school to work harder than ever on his many jobs.

✽ ✽ ✽

In May, 1895 Grand Army Posts all over the country were protesting against the desecration of Memorial Day by racing, baseball games, and so forth.

"Memorial Day is more sacred than the Sabbath to many of the old veterans and they want it sacredly observed," said one of the GAR members.

The Clyde Baseball Club ignored the request.

"What's so sinful about baseball on Decoration Day?" one of the Clyde Stars asked.

The team was scheduled to play their first game of the season against Tiffin at Ames Field on that day. A backstop and a grand stand had been erected there. The boys were in high glee over the generous action of Z. Taylor, the dry-goods king, who donated handsome suits for the club at a cost of $75.

Sherwood was too busy. Harry Surbeck was now the manager. Barley Mann was pitcher. Waxey Sellinger, who had moved back to Clyde, was catcher. Toughy McCreery, first base; Herman Hurd, shortstop, and other members were on the team.

Sherwood and some of the other young men joined the McPherson Guard. They drilled and paraded around town. It was fun, good exercise and paid a little.

✽ ✽ ✽

A year after the disastrous fire in the Dewey block, another close call came. The fire department was on the ground almost simultaneously with the alarm. The hose was attached and before the fire had a chance to spread, the danger was over.

As with every type of excitement in town, Sherwood took a look at the damage done to the Dewey block. His friend, Johnny Botsford was also checking it out.

"Seems like they just got this place fixed up from last year's fire," he said.

Johnny worked at *The Reporter* office, a rival of *The Clyde Enterprise*. The two chatted for a few minutes. Sherwood noticed Johnny's badly swollen arm and hand. He asked him what happened.

"Blood poisoning," Johnny said. "My hand was already sore, and with handling type, it got infected."

He asked Sherwood about his work at the *Enterprise*. Sherwood told him he was in and out.

❋ ❋ ❋

Modern businesses were coming to Clyde. The organ factory had become a piano factory. The piano factory had closed and now a bicycle factory took its place. Sherwood got a job in the enamel shed at the factory. Little skill was involved and the work was not heavy, but it was tiring. Sherwood worked twelve hours a day. The process of dipping and brushing and baking was endless and boring. The fumes stung Sherwood's eyes and nose. His throat burned. His head throbbed.

❋ ❋ ❋

The Sun Bros. Circus came to town on May 15th, 1896. This company had been in Clyde before and always gave the best twenty-five cent show on the road.

A ludicrous incident occurred during the parade. Just before the parade left the show grounds to make the tour of the town, a woebegone stranger driving an old sway-back nag pulling a rickety wagon with a chicken crate in the back had broken down across Forest Street exactly in the way of the on-coming parade.

A crowd had gathered to watch the parade and many smiled at the stranger wondering how he was going to get his rig out of the way of the parade.

"He looks like he had come out of the wilds of Seneca County, sold his load of chickens and was now going to get a free glimpse of an elephant before he went on home." One of the parade viewers said.

He was an odd looking character. An old straw hat sat on the back of his head, a stream of Battle Ax tobacco juice trickled from each corner of his mouth. His pantaloons ended halfway between his knees and ankles, and displayed a pair of gorgeous red stockings when he elevated his feet onto the dashboard.

Gus Sun, one of the owners, and a loud-mouthed individual, who announced the attraction of the circus led the procession in a single buggy. After a good deal of maneuvering and a few cuss words, they succeeded in getting by the backwoods obstruction.

The bandwagon with six horses came next and was unable to get by. The driver argued and swore. Gus Sun turned around and came back to deal with the obstructionist. The whole parade came to a standstill.

"Get out of the way!"

"Take a wheel off his wagon!"

"Go on, you galoot!"

"I'll knock him down wid a hammer," yelled John Enright.

Finally, fearing some violence, a mild-eyed, meek-mannered Main Street businessman, who was standing by, took the old nag by the bridle and led him out of the way.

The procession proceeded. Once more the old farmer turned his outfit directly in the way of the next four-horse team. The driver of this lost his patience and slashed his long-lashed whip back and forth finally getting him out of the way.

The incident was supposed to be closed until a few minutes later when at the "grand free exhibition" at the end of the parade, the onlookers all gasped with delight.

This same backwoods galoot walked out to the tight-wire and stripped off his farmer's garb. Underneath he wore a brilliant set of scarlet tights. He was one of the circus performers and one of the best tight-wire walkers ever seen in Clyde. The crowd whooped and hollered and clapped their hands. They were surprised, amazed and delighted to have been bamboozled.

The mild-eyed, meek-mannered businessman, who out of the goodness of his heart had led the brute out of the way of the procession, received congratulations from his friends. He was embarrassed by the entire incident.

The crowd was huge. The boys of the town were delighted with the performance.

The Clyde Boys

In St. Louis, Missouri, June 18, 1896, Republicans nominated William McKinley on the first ballot. The crowd went wild. State standards were uprooted and carried up and down the aisles by shrieking delegates. Hundreds of women in the galleries fluttered their handkerchiefs. The uproar lasted twelve minutes.

There was plenty of McKinley enthusiasm in Clyde. The town was a genuine bedlam for several hours. In the vicinity of the *Enterprise* office the enthusiasm ran so high, or the youngsters' dynamite crackers produced such a concussion that a big window in the rear of the office was broken.

❋ ❋ ❋

Misses Nellie and Edith Heffner, daughters of the auctioneer, gave a Halloween Party at their Buckeye Street home. They sent out unique invitations to come at seven in the evening and woe to anyone who is late.

About fifty young people attended and were met at the door by a ghost. Jack o'lanterns were stationed here and there. The guests spent the evening in the performance of spells to drive away witches, and to discover their future partners for life. The gentlemen retired to a room, while the ladies arrayed themselves in ghost costumes. The gentlemen then selected their partners from the ghosts. Many were the surprises when the identity was discovered.

The elegant refreshments were served on cabbage leaves. Old time fireside revelries were enjoyed such as popping of chestnuts in the fire.

"What a great party," one of the girls' old classmates said, "We've come a long way from tossing cabbages."

❋ ❋ ❋

Jennie Bemis, who had been in Chicago, arrived in Clyde the first part of June, 1897 to spend the summer with her mother. Cliff, who had moved back to Clyde, was glad to see her.

Cliff told her about Frank Baker's Model Bakery and they walked down to Railroad Street for a dish of ice cream. Herman Hurd was there.

"What a surprise," Cliff said.

Frank came over to take their order. "I've added something new in the way of a good drink. DeVita Soft Drinks, all flavors, made with DeVita mineral water. Sold by the bottle or glass. Would you like to try it?"

Jennie and Cliff laughed. "He's quite the salesman," Cliff said, "But we came for ice cream."

Jennie Baker came out of the back room and squealed when she saw Jennie Bemis.

"The two Jennie B's are together again," Herman Hurd said.

The four gathered around a table with ice cream. "Seems like old times," Cliff said, "But now you are the owners."

The talk got around to Karl and Sherwood.

"Old Jobby and I used to come in here. Jennie was here. Her mom would get us a dish of ice cream and two spoons."

Herman laughed uproariously at the thought.

❋ ❋ ❋

Smoky Pete, began celebrating the Fourth on Saturday, July 3rd. About midnight Sunday, he became gloriously drunk, and was gathered in by the police. He sweltered in the cooler all day Monday and on Tuesday morning pleaded guilty to drunkenness before Mayor Sprague and was fined $5 and costs, which he paid.

Monday, July 5th, Harriett Day, Jennie Baker, Herman Hurd, Will Tiffany and about eight others spent the day at Wightman's Grove on the Sandusky Bay. Will Tiffany was the only ambitious one in the crowd, catching several hundred pounds of fish. The weather was blistering hot and Jennie was glad to be out of the bakery.

❋ ❋ ❋

A couple of longhaired short pantalooned fellows came to town Saturday afternoon advertising the Cleveland Bicycle. They wheeled in and started in on the performance of expert trick riding on Main Street. Soon quite a crowd gathered. The duo performed some difficult feats. The crowd clapped as they finished their performance.

Sixteen year old Harry Heffner, who was in the crowd, mounted his Outing, and for half an hour duplicated their tricks, performed many others much more difficult and outdid the visitors in every way.

They got mad and left in a huff. Harry was heartily applauded. The fellows had no idea of meeting such a performer in a town like this.

❋ ❋ ❋

On Wednesday afternoon, November 24th 1897, Jennie Baker and Herman Hurd quietly slipped over to

Bellevue. At five o'clock, in St. Paul's Episcopal Church, Rev. E.S. Doan married the couple.

They returned to Clyde the same evening and set up housekeeping in a suite of rooms over the *Enterprise* office.

"The store is closed on Thanksgiving," Herman said, "So I'll have the day off."

* * *

Smoky Pete had been fairly quiet lately. Ben Jackson, the editor commented: "Pete has purchased a new turnout and he's now cutting quite a swell on the streets. It isn't exactly a landau, nor a hansom, nor yet a tally-ho, but Pete says it's more useful than any of these, if not as ornamental. He drives an indirect descendent of Hambletonian 10 to the gig, and will use it to cart offal from the streets, and incidentally to earn an odd dime in draying.

"What do you do with the stuff you haul off Main Street?" a citizen asked Pete after he watched him fill his wagon with street scrapings.

Pete laughed. "Why I repair Buckeye Street with it," he said.

"Buckeye looks as though you've worked on it for some time," the citizen said.

In early January 1898 there had been around 200 skaters, young and old at the Waterworks Pond. Many from the country had driven in, left their wraps and blankets at the pumping house and joined in the sport until midnight. The ice had been good and the skating was fine. About the most graceful skater in the crowd so far was Attorney Tom Dewey, who had been taking lessons from his son, Ben.

✳ ✳ ✳

A telephone was installed in the Union School building.

There were now 118 instruments connected with this exchange in Clyde. Miss Sarah Suggitt, who had taught some of the boys at the Union School, operated the telephone exchange. She was talking to a friend about her work.

"One day recently when the exchange was not very busy, I kept track of the number of calls sent in. They numbered over a thousand!"

"That's a lot of conversations," said her friend, "This indicates that the exchange is the medium for doing a good deal of business or a good deal of gossiping, or both."

✳ ✳ ✳

In January 1898 the Battleship Maine was ordered to Havana. Supposedly, the ship was on a courtesy visit. Many believed it was there to protect American citizens from civil disorders.

On February 15th, the Maine was fired upon. This set in motion the final moves, which preceded the declaration of war.

At the *Morning Telegram* offices in New York City, where he had moved after finishing his schooling at the Art Institute of Chicago, Karl gathered his resources quickly and made a drawing illustrating "The Blowing Up of the Maine," His illustration was printed on the cover of the Sunday edition.

At the same time, the *New York Journal* published diagrams showing how the bomb, the "infernal machine" had been placed, which blew up the battleship.

The entire country was in an uproar over this. Would there be a war? Memories of the Civil War were still fresh in the minds of old veterans. They didn't want to see their sons march off to battle.

Sherwood and Irve had moved to Chicago when Karl still lived there, obtaining jobs in a cold storage warehouse and attending school. Sherwood mulled the Maine disaster over in his mind. He was not happy with his classes at the Lewis Institute. He couldn't seem to get ahead. He was still a member of the McPherson Guard. He wrote a letter to Captain William E. Gillett in Clyde:

Captain Gillett:
Dear Sir:
If by any chance this war scare amounts to anything, And the company is called please telegraph me at 708 Michigan Boulevard and I will be with you.
Sherwood Anderson, Chicago, Ill.

There was a long column in the *Enterprise* titled, "Soldiers Ready for Service." Ben Jackson, the editor, wrote that while the boys of our local military were not exactly itching for war, they felt that since the Spaniards blew up our battleship they must well pay for it or fight. They had seen service during the Cincinnati riots, the Wheeling strike and other times to know that war is serious.

There were around fifty men of Company I, 16th Regiment, O.N.G. Sherwood was one of them. Captain Gillett received several letters from members of his unit. One was from a Green Spring fellow asking if he could be a drummer. Gillett showed the letters to Ben Jackson and he published them.

After Sherwood wrote to Captain Gillett, he settled back with his loathsome job to await orders.

Cliff breezed back to Chicago toward the end of March for a week's visit. Sherwood asked him how his preaching was coming along. Cliff told him all the advantages and disadvantages of the profession.

"But I'm still very much into the ministry," he told Sherwood.

He was on vacation from Oberlin College. The school was closed and he came to Chicago with other friends.

* * *

Smoky Pete had been on his good behavior for a while. Now he was in trouble again. He said he was the victim of "circumstances." He was arrested on a warrant sworn out by William Giles, charging him with using bad language on the public streets.

"He'll be given a hearing." The mayor said, "Pete has been suffering from a bad case of alcoholism for a couple of weeks and should be given a chance to sober up."

They confined him in Brown's Hotel. In some mysterious manner, Pete secured a crowbar. He broke a hole in the roof and escaped.

"Somebody said he was seen in Sandusky," one of the citizens reported. "Pete hasn't a very good opinion of Mayor Sprague. So I suspect when the new mayor Richards takes his seat, Pete will return."

Another agreed. "If the authorities could only find the fellow who gave Pete the crowbar, they would be willing to let Pete take up his abode elsewhere."

S.D. West identified the crowbar as one that was stolen from his blacksmith shop a year or more ago.

On Friday, April 15th, Mayor-elect Richards and the other newly elected village officers took the oath of office. As the townspeople predicted, after Richards was sworn in as mayor, Smoky Pete returned to Clyde. He had been hiding for a couple of weeks. He was again taken into custody where he awaited his hearing.

His hearing was on Thursday, April 21st before Mayor Richards. He pleaded not guilty and conducted his own defense,

"I fail to believe your story," said His Honor.

Pete was found guilty and fined $10 and costs, a total of $20.30. In default of payment he was sent back to jail.

"Poor Pete, he still languishes in jail," said a citizen. "I wish he'd get out. Main Street needs a good cleaning."

❈ ❈ ❈

The American fleet forced its way past the forts and into the mined harbor of Manila, the Spanish capital, where it anchored and prepared to bombard the city.

May 1st, 1898, Commander George Dewey gave the command: "You may fire when you are ready, Gridley," and an American naval force destroyed the Spanish fleet in Manila Bay.

The boys of Company I had arrived in Columbus, Ohio at 2:30 a.m. on Friday, April 29th. They marched six miles to the campgrounds and were tired.

When the boys got to the camp nothing was ready. There were no tents. When they finally got tents and got them put up it was after 7:30. There was no straw for ticks and the ground was damp. Most of the company went uptown and stayed there all night.

"The boys do not seem to like the life of a soldier, but would rather be at home in their little beds," Mack Robinson said.

Sherwood smiled. He had spent many nights on the ground when he was in the stables. Of course there was straw in the stables, but it still wasn't as comfortable as most of his comrades' beds.

Taps sounded at 9:30 p.m. and reveille was at five in the morning. In between there were drills, school, dress parade, and sunset retreat.

Sunday, May 1st, William Gillett was the Captain of the provost guard at Camp Bushnell. He was on duty twenty-four hours in that capacity. With 90 men, 11 from Company I with Corporal Mack Dennis arrested four pickpockets.

"There were more pickpockets here than there was in Clyde at the time of the unveiling of the McPherson monument," said one of the boys.

Mack Dennis felt very big since he arrested the pickpockets and thought he would run for Second Lieutenant if there were a chance.

"He thinks he deserves a Colonel's position," his friend said.

By May 4th, the boys were in a regular routine and were drilling twice a day. They drilled by bugle calls in battle formation.

"Some of the boys don't like the bill of fare, but have to put up with it," one said.

"Fat pork, eggs, a little beef, and also pork and beans," another said, "It's filling."

They were talking to Ben Jackson from the *Enterprise*, who went to Columbus to see first hand how the boys were doing. Ben received a cordial invitation from Captain Gillett to have dinner with the boys. The dinner consisted of beefsteak, boiled potatoes, bread and butter, gravy, and black coffee.

Ben reported to the folks back home, "Those people who are worrying about the soldier boys in camp not having enough to eat are wasting their sympathy," Ben said, "The boys don't get chicken, pie and cake every day, but they do have plenty of good wholesome food, and Joel Elliott is a first class cook."

The other companies envied the Clyde boys. They thought they had the best of everything as they had that fine cooking range and also had oilcloth for their tables. The other companies didn't even have a table.

❊ ❊ ❊

Barley Mann and Willie Sargeant ran barbershops and they made a rule that they would not shave any mustaches.

The boys spent most of their free time playing checkers, writing to their girl-friends and sleeping.

Sherwood read. Just as he had done in Johnny Becker's tailor shop, he scrounged around and found whatever he could to read, dime novels, Harpers' Weekly, Leslie's Weekly and others. He also did a little writing to girls.

❋ ❋ ❋

Karl made several trips to Mechanic Street to see the Bardshars.

"Henry joined Teddy Roosevelt's regiment of Rough Riders," Ruth Bardshar said. "He enlisted at Whipple Barracks on the first of May. He was one of the first to sign up."

"That's Henry," Karl said, "Looking for action."

Ruth had fixed a cup of tea for Karl. They were in the spacious kitchen of the comfortable home. Birdie joined them.

"Henry's been at Prescott, Arizona in the mines," Ruth said, "When the call came, there was no holding Henry back. He's in the Cavalry."

Ruth was proud and very worried.

"Mother's afraid Henry will get hurt," Birdie said.

"Killed," Ruth said, "You can say it."

"Not Henry," Karl said. "Henry will survive." He took a sip of his tea and picked up a cookie. "Stella is worried sick about Sherwood. Sherwood is another one out looking for adventure."

The men who went to war put up with their hardships and discomforts. But they joked about some if their irritations. Mack Lemmon said he had to peel potatoes all day long.

And then there was a sad day. May 11th. George Burton Meek was killed. He was the captain of a one-pounder rapid-fire gun on the Winslow, which was a torpedo boat. Word reached Clyde and the town was draped in sadness.

He was the first to be killed in the service of the United States in the War with Spain. Bert Meek was 26 years old.

❋ ❋ ❋

Camp George H. Thomas, Chickamauga Park, Georgia, was a historic battlefield. Thirty-five years ago there was a terrible conflict on that spot and nearly 30,000 men lost their lives. In June 1898, 50,000 Volunteers gathered there from nearly every state.

Now tenting side by side were regiments from both the North and the South drilling on the same field. They were the sons of those in the '63 battle. The song, "Tenting on the Old Camp Ground" was very timely with the boys from Company I.

Each day five to seven men from a company were permitted to visit Chattanooga and points of interest in that vicinity. One was Lookout Mountain where one could see into five different states from the top of it.

One day Sargeant Sellinger, Corporal Robinson, Musician Caddie Ford, Barley Mann and Willie Sargeant went to Chattanooga. They had supper at the Rossmore Hotel, which was kept by Mrs. Nelson, formerly Mrs. Jennie Reed of the Nichols House of Clyde.

"It's a small world," the boys all agreed.

They feasted their eyes on the view from Lookout Mountain, the natural scenery, the view of the city and the river winding for forty miles.

Sherwood made the trip the following day with several other privates and Sargeant Lemmon. And like all the others, who gazed across the landscape from Lookout Mountain, he was filled with awe.

Georgia was hot. The men had salt pork and hard tack and had not been used to that kind of army grub. With too much grease in such hot weather, many got sick. Nothing serious. Sherwood managed the meals and the heat.

When he began to think he was suffering with the heat and when he began to feel miserable, he thought about the cold storage and he whistled a happy tune. He didn't admit it, but he enjoyed parts of his army life.

Sherwood was an outdoor fellow. He had no fear of spiders, small garter snakes or lizards. There was a rumor that lizards abounded in camp. Joel Elliott, who was the camp cook, said he was not afraid of lizards. Sherwood and the others knew otherwise.

One evening before taps when the young soldiers were sitting about, Sherwood, Barley Mann, Charlie Dennis, Willie Sargeant, Joel Elliott and others, talking about lizards.

"Like I said, I'm not afraid of lizards," Joel Elliott said.

Joel didn't notice Sherwood, who was sitting beside him. But the others did. Sherwood wet his finger and put it on Joel's neck.

Joel leaped up and grabbed the back of his neck.

"I thought he was going through the top of the tent!" one of the fellows said.

After Joel calmed down, he began searching all over for lizards in the tent.

"Go to bed, Joel," the tent mates pleaded.

"Not until I've searched every inch of this place," Joel said.

After Captain William Gillett was promoted to Major, he purchased a horse. The horse wouldn't stand still on dress parade. Major Gillett wanted to quiet him so the next day he rode him to Chattanooga, nine miles away.

"He's a little frisky when we get out to drill, but he's a fine-looking animal and gentle," one of the men said.

"I think he will get over the friskiness when Major Gillett has used him a few times," another said.

At Chickamauga Park, the YMCA of Ohio had put up a large tent just a few steps from the camp. Sunday services were held at the tent by the Chaplain and were largely attended.

"I understand the businessmen of Ohio are paying for this," one of the men said.

"That's what I hear," was the answer.

There were long tables with pens, ink, writing papers and envelopes. There were tables with checkerboards. There was a reading room with books, magazines and newspapers.

"Nobody spends more time at the YMCA tent than Jobby Anderson," several of the men said.

There was a canteen across from the YMCA where they dispensed beer and tobacco. The boys got a certain number of chips to spend on tobacco, but none for beer.

Sherwood didn't mind most of the routine work around the camp. He took part in the horseplay and enjoyed the camaraderie of his fellow servicemen. He and Joel Elliott reminisced about Clyde, and the people back home.

"We seem to be playthings," Joel said, "Allowed about one half government rations, not so much as we like, tooted into bed with a single bugle every night, and routed out every morning with the same instrument of torture.

Sherwood nodded, but said nothing. Joel went on.

"Remember, I recognize the necessity of discipline, but I never was used to this before and it seems different.

Sherwood agreed.

"I miss Frank Welker," Joel said, "I wish I could visit him and get some of those glorious lunches that haunt my dreams."

Sherwood's mind drifted. He remembered his late afternoons with Julia Welker in the Empire House kitchen and a generous slab of warm apple pie and a cool glass of milk.

"I would trade Frank and Julia a whole side of sow belly for a leg of chicken," Joel said.

A young lady gave the boys of Company I a little dog. They named him Tampa.

Rumors abounded that the 6th Regiment would be sent to Tampa, Florida.

"Not so," one of the men learned "Our Colonel will not take us there. He said the water was bad, and we just came from a cool climate, and it would never do."

Major Gillett thought they would be sent west. As it was, he didn't know either.

✵ ✵ ✵

In the meantime, the Rough Riders were already in Santiago de Cuba. Henry Bardshar wrote his mother and word was passed back to those in Company I.

"At least Henry is on the move," one of the boys said. "Leave it to Henry to get into the action."

After the quartermaster wrote to the Ladies Aid about the need for socks and hospital gowns, the society bustled about and prepared boxes. They shipped a carload of items to the boys at Chickamauga.

Eleven wagons rolled into camp. There was a large banner on the wagons marked, "Carload of Square Meals."

"J.B. Tichenor's work, " remarked one of the boys when he saw the banner.

It seemed more like a crowd of children around a Christmas tree than anything else. The boys all gathered around and as the boxes were opened, each one was handed his packages. Such feasts as the boys enjoyed with the canned fruits and other goodies put smiles on the faces of the boys at Company I.

❋ ❋ ❋

It was July when the Bardshars in Clyde finally heard from their Rough Rider son, Henry.

"There were two letters this week," William Bardshar reported to friends. "They were written in June."

Not only letters, but Henry had sent a war memento home to his family.

"It's gruesome, " Bardshar said as he displayed it around town. "It's a Mauser bullet such as used in the Spanish guns and Henry said it was one of the first articles captured in the fight. He was in the thick of the Battle of Santiago."

The old veterans of the town handled the relic and passed it from one to another.

"Henry said the weather was very hot. He was sea sick on the ship sixteen days."

"He's all right now?" an onlooker asked.

"He's fine, but their horses haven't arrived." He laughed. "Henry said thanks to the poor marksmanship of the Spanish, no one was hurt."

On July 1st from 4 a.m. without rest the Rough Riders fought on the battlefield at Santiago. Henry wrote his mother on July 4th that he was now the aide-de-camp to Colonel Roosevelt.

"You will see that I have done my duty and you will get all the news from the papers," Henry wrote.

❋ ❋ ❋

The newspapers reported the death of Captain Bucky O'Neill. He was strolling up and down in front of his men smoking a cigarette. One of the sergeants said, "Captain, a bullet is sure to hit you."

O'Neill took the cigarette out of his mouth, blew a cloud of smoke and laughed.

He said, "Sergeant, the Spanish bullet isn't made that will kill me."

A moment later, he turned on his heel and was fatally shot.

When O'Neill was killed, Henry Bardshar immediately attached himself to Colonel Roosevelt as his orderly.

❋ ❋ ❋

Sherwood and the boys were greatly disappointed. Company I of the Sixth Regiment was still at Chickamauga. The order for them to move was countermanded.

"We could be here for weeks," one said, "or even months!"

They had expected to leave for Puerto Rico and were getting in shape for a march. They had heard the news about Santiago and yelled themselves hoarse. Bands played and firecrackers were shot off.

"Are they happy about Santiago?" one asked, "I think they're happy it's pay day."

They received their pay, which had been delayed due to one problem or another, and they also received a box from Clyde Ladies Soldiers Aid Society.

"Look at that!" the boys exclaimed when the box was opened. It contained over 700 magazines and 92 novels. No one was happier than Sherwood.

❋ ❋ ❋

On Sunday, August 14th, Colonel Roosevelt and his Rough Riders steamed through the still waters of the Sound and cast anchor off Montauk Point, Long Island.

Many of the men had yellow fever. Henry had been well nearly all the while he was in Cuba. He came through the battles unscathed by Spanish bullets, but when he went with his regiment to Montauk Point, he was taken sick with malarial fever.

Colonel Roosevelt, himself, reported that Henry Bardshar was a wreck, literally at death's door. He had lost over eighty pounds and was a mere skeleton.

But Henry kept the news of his ill health from his mother. At least he tried to.

"I don't want to worry her, Henry said, "She worries enough as it is."

It isn't clear how it happened, but Henry was moved to the home of his aunt and uncle in New York City to recuperate.

"You're thin, Henry," Aunt Eliza said, "But your mother will expect that. At least you're not the ghostly phantom I saw when you first came to New York."

When Henry was able to walk without assistance, he made arrangements to go home. He arrived in Clyde on September 26th. At the same time he received a letter from Teddy Roosevelt, his old commander.

"He wants me to visit him at Oyster Bay," Henry said.

"Sagamore Hill?" his mother gasped.

His sister Birdie was impressed. "It's huge, Henry. Three floors, twenty-two rooms. I've seen pictures."

"I'm anxious to see his trophy room," Henry said.

Henry remembered too, what the Colonel had told all his men.

"The world will be kind to you for about ten days. For just ten days you will be over-praised, over petted and then you will find that the hero-business is over for good and all. If you try to trade any longer on this, you will merely excite laughter or derision."

But Henry, being Henry, was in a way like the Major. He couldn't help telling his war stories.

How he shared his blanket with Colonel Teddy. How he made bunks of bamboo for the Colonel whenever they changed camp. How Colonel Teddy nearly lost his revolver, a prized possession from the sunken battleship Maine. How he saved Teddy's life by shooting two Spaniards who ambushed them.

Henry didn't stop being a hero after ten days.

In October 1898, Company I was firmly settled at Camp Poland in Knoxville, Tennessee. It was a scenic spot, nestled among mountains in the Tennessee River Valley.

Sherwood had been promoted to Corporal in July, along with Mack Dennis and C. M. McCleary. The boys of Company I enjoyed the food, which was better than at Chickamauga Park. The tents had floors in them and they had ticks to sleep on.

Many of the boys were sick and had been sent home to recuperate. Joel Elliot was in Clyde after he became ill. Pat Waddams took his place in camp as cook.

Company I had been fortunate in the matter of fatalities and hoped that all Clyde soldiers would pass through their term of service unscathed. But Fate intervened and there was a death.

Frank Craig died at his parents' home near Galetown on October 5th. He had come home the last day of August, suffering from typhoid fever and the results of a severe attack of measles.

Willie Sargeant and Harkness Miller also came home on sick leave with him.

Major William Gillett had been on a leave of absence. He had been under the weather himself, but spent most of his leave time visiting the sick boys who were home from camp.

Gillett attended the funeral of Private Craig on Friday, October 7th and on Saturday, he returned to Knoxville.

The funeral of the late Frank Craig was the largest that had taken place in the community since the burial of Judge John M. Lemmon. There were over 250 carriages in the vicinity and it was impossible for all those present to get near enough to the house to hear the services.

✱ ✱ ✱

Company 1 had finally arrived in Cuba as part of the Sixth Ohio Regiment. The soldiers were camped on an old sugar plantation along the railroad to Santa Clara. One day Sherwood, Harry Sargent and Lt. Jesse Douglas went exploring. They were looking for war mementos at an old fort. The men poked around and gathered up some things to take back. They came out into the sunlight and shielded their eyes.

"What are those things on me?" Harry asked Lt. Douglas.

Some kind of insects were crawling and creeping and flitting over his uniform.

"Fleas!" Douglas said. He looked at his own uniform. "I will bet there are about a million!"

Sherwood hopped about and brushed his uniform. The fleas bit Sherwood and he slapped at them. He whipped off his shirt and flapped it to try to get rid of them.

"Fleas up north don't bite," Douglas said, "But these fleas keep me guessing."

"I don't think I want to come back to this fort," Harry said.

Sherwood laughed. "Me neither," he said.

❋ ❋ ❋

The April 1899 number of *Scribner's* magazine featured an article, "The Cavalry at Santiago," by Theodore Roosevelt, Governor of New York and ex-colonel of the Rough Riders. Colonel Roosevelt was contributing a series of articles to *Scribner's* about the campaign in Cuba.

"Would you look at this?" was the echo in Clyde, in Springfield where Karl had moved after a short time in New York, even in Sagua La Grande, Cuba, where Company 1 was now stationed.

In the article, Roosevelt paid a glowing tribute to the bravery and valor of his orderly, Henry Bardshar.

In Clyde, William Bardshar had a copy of the magazine. Several lawyers, doctors and merchants had a copy or saw an issue.

In Springfield at "The Oaks," Mrs. Folger kept the latest magazines of national interest in her parlor for the benefit of her guests. Karl saw one and showed it to Stella and their brother Earl who were living at the rooming house as well.

"Well, I guess old Henry didn't make up all those tales he told when he got back," Karl said, "Teddy Roosevelt wouldn't lie about how Henry saved his life."

In Cuba, Sherwood had come off guard duty when he saw the magazine in the library area. Company I's reading material was outdated when it got to camp, but someone, somehow acquired this late issue.

Sherwood, who read everything he could find, to begin with, sat down and read the entire article. He let out a yelp and his soldier comrades came running. Sherwood held up the *Scribner's* magazine.

"Look here," Sherwood said. "Our old friend Henry Bardshar is a hero."

The others gathered around to see what the Colonel had written.

"Good old Henry," Sherwood said, "He wanted adventure. He got it."

"And here we sit bored to pieces," one of the others said.

❋ ❋ ❋

June 6th, 1899 Clyde was anticipating the Company I banquet at the Armory. Committees had been appointed weeks ago and the decorations and food preparations had been going on since the first announcement. Now, at last, the day had come and with it, torrid heat.

"Hah, just like the weather we left," one of the tanned and bronzed Company I soldiers said with a laugh.

The reception began at eight o'clock at the K of P Hall just across the entry from the Armory Hall where the banquet was spread. The guests consisted of the soldiers, their relatives and friends. Hundreds of the friends of the soldiers were unable to gain admission to the hall.

The reception committee welcomed the soldiers and each guest was furnished a neat ribbon badge. Close's Orchestra played patriotic music for the guests. They spent a pleasant hour devoted to exchange of greetings and then the doors of the banquet room were thrown open and the scene was breathtaking.

The hall was festooned with flags and bunting. The stage was completely hidden beneath folds of a large American flag. Smaller flags were everywhere.

Tables were adorned with flowers and arranged so that two-hundred and fifty could be seated at once.

The menu consisted of the choicest viands, fried chicken, veal loaf, cold ham, potato salad, deviled eggs, white and brown bread and desserts of ice cream, cake, strawberries, oranges, bananas and nuts. And of course drinks of coffee, tea or milk.

Thirty-six young ladies acted as waiters. The Hurd sisters, Hattie Dewey, Mabel Pawsey and Ina Adare were among them.

Homer Metzgar, the attorney, was Master of Ceremonies and Reverend William Kepler invoked the blessing. The orchestra came in and occupied the stage and rendered several choice selections while supper was in progress.

During the supper the doors were opened to the crowd of spectators who wished to hear the speeches, and the rear of the hall was jammed with people. Toastmaster Metzgar opened the toasts.

Major William Gillett was called upon and he begged to be excused and said he knew Chaplain McConnell would speak for him. There were many speeches and frequent applause.

"The Roll of Honor" was the last toast of the evening. It was responded to briefly by J.B. Sprague, who spoke with feeling of the deaths of Frank Craig and John Ward of Company I, Harry Knowles of the regular army and George B. Meek of the Navy.

Dancing completed the evening festivities. Needless to say Sherwood enjoyed himself thoroughly. He chatted and listened to plans of his comrades.

"What do you plan to do now?" was a frequently asked question.

"I'm starting Thursday at Ramsey's Barber Shop," Willie Sargeant said to Sherwood, and Sherwood told him of his plans to visit in Springfield.

Sherwood traded adventures, danced and had a relaxing evening.

"The only thing that would have made this evening better, would have been a cooling breeze," said one of the soldiers.

* * *

The Spring term at Oberlin College closed. Cliff Paden and his cousin, Dean Richmond were home for the summer vacation. They planned to spend the time in Clyde.

Cliff lost no time getting into a special project. He had completed arrangements whereby the members of Grace Episcopal Sunday School would have access to a library of over a thousand volumes.

"Cliff, what a terrific idea," one of the members said to him.

"I've thought about it a long time," Cliff said, "The books would be free to members of the Sunday School to borrow. Those outside the Sunday School may borrow books with a fee of five cents for two weeks."

Cliff had pondered the problem of such little reading material in a town the size of Clyde. Since he had been to Chicago, and to Oberlin where both places had libraries, he had devised a plan to put books in his own Grace Episcopal Church.

The library came in sections of fifty volumes each and the first section had already been put in place. The books were new, of the best editions, well bound and selected for all ages.

"You going to get 'David Harum', Cliff?' one of the members asked.

Cliff laughed. "Now, you will just have to wait and see, won't you?"

'David Harum' written by Edward Noyes Wescott was one of the greatest selling books written in recent years.

※ ※ ※

In December 1899, Sherwood was in Springfield, Ohio with Karl.

"Hah!" Sherwood said. He was reading a letter from Jennie Hurd. "Barley Mann and Willie Sargeant opened their new barber shop over in Canada."

Main Street north of Buckeye was called Canada.

Karl looked up. Sherwood laughed. "Sure hope they've improved their hair-cuts since they cut hair in Cuba."

Karl was absorbed in a letter from one of his artist friends, but he was constantly interrupted by Sherwood's shrieks.

Jennie's letter was long and newsy and every paragraph or so, Sherwood would relate some item of interest to Karl.

"I could just read the letter myself," Karl said.

Sherwood laughed.

✻ ✻ ✻

During the fall of 1900, all across the country, Election Fever was accelerating. McKinley and Roosevelt headed the Republican ticket. McKinley was bidding for his second term and Theodore Roosevelt was the nominee for Vice President.

On October 17th, Theodore Roosevelt was in Clyde, Ohio. There was a very large crowd in Clyde, along with several hundred strong of the McKinley Club, who wore yellow ribbon badges. The area around the station fluttered with flags. The Hughes Granite and Marble Works were profusely decorated for the occasion. The Clyde Cornet Band livened the station area with music. "There'll be a Hot Time in the Old Town Tonight," was a favorite tune.

Before Colonel Roosevelt spoke he requested that Mr. and Mrs. William Bardshar come to the car so he could meet them. Henry's father and sister, Miss Bertha, were in the crowd and came forward. Governor Roosevelt greeted them warmly, almost affectionately.

William Bardshar, just past 83 years old, expressed regret that Mrs. Bardshar was too ill to leave home.

"I wanted to meet the father of my brave adjutant," Roosevelt said, as he clasped Bardshar around the shoulders.

And to Birdie, he said, "I frequently read the letters you wrote to Henry." He laughed his Roosevelt barking laugh, "I enjoyed them thoroughly."

Roosevelt, in his address, spoke in highest terms of Henry Bardshar, his fellow-soldier in Cuba. His speech was not long, but showed a surprising knowledge of Clyde and its affairs. He complimented Clyde on its wonderfully patriotic record in sending soldiers to the front.

He closed with an appeal for support of the Republican ticket in the coming election. The Bardshars, along with the crowds from Clyde swelled with pride and applauded wildly.

"I believe I'm about the happiest man in the world, right now," William Bardshar said to Birdie.

❋ ❋ ❋

For years Karl had planned to go to Europe to study art. He had saved his money religiously. Then there would come a crisis in the family. He would help out, deplete his funds, and slowly start replacing the spent savings. He felt he could leave the country now with everything taken care of and no guilt.

Especially no guilt since he had given Stella a packet of a thousand dollars. He definitely could use the money himself, but to pass it on to Stella relieved him temporarily of family responsibility, at least until he returned.

Karl smiled when he thought of how surprised Stella was when she peeked inside the envelope.

This year, 1900, he finally had enough money to live and work and study in Paris. And so, on October 19th, he sailed for Europe.

Later Years

Through the years, the boys of Clyde who moved away returned again for visits and reunions and to dip their feet again in 'Coon Creek.

The Anderson brothers, Henry Bardshar and Cliff Paden had left Clyde by the 1900s. Karl Anderson moved to Westport Connecticut, became a well-known artist with paintings in museums across the United States. Sherwood Anderson became a writer. His most famous work was *Winesburg Ohio*. Cliff Paden changed his name to John Emerson, became a movie director and married Anita Loos, known for her book *Gentlemen Prefer Blondes*. In 1936 he produced and directed the movie *San Francisco*. Henry Bardshar remained in the West. He was actively involved in the government of the Western Territories during the formation of the new states of Arizona and New Mexico. Herman Hurd remained in Clyde and operated his father's grocery store. He was elected to the Clyde Board of Education and became its president. The Grace Episcopal Church is now the Clyde Museum, the home of the Clyde Heritage League.

www.ingramcontent.com/pod-product-compliance
Lightning Source LLC
Chambersburg PA
CBHW031420290426
44110CB00011B/462